It's All About The Value

Improving Sales Effectiveness for Small Businesses

Phil Sayers

To Steve.

Enjoy!!

Phil Sayers

It’s All About The Value

First published 2018

This book is not intended to provide personalised legal, financial or investment advice. The author specifically disclaims any liability, loss or risk which is incurred as a consequence, directly or indirectly of the use and application of any of the content of this work.

Author: Phil Sayers

CONTENTS

Introduction

Who is this book for?

Chapter 1. It's all about the value

Chapter 2. So where do we start?

Chapter 3. Who should we be selling to?

Chapter 4. The competition

Chapter 5. How do customers buy?

Chapter 6. Elevator pitches

Chapter 7. Starting to sell

Chapter 8. Making the first call / meeting

Chapter 9. SPIN® Selling

Chapter 10. Presentations and product demonstrations

Chapter 11. Closing

Chapter 12. Handling objections

Chapter 13. Negotiation

Chapter 14. Quotes and proposals

Chapter 15. Account management

Chapter 16. Sales activity

Chapter 17. CRM systems

Chapter 18. Sales commission

Chapter 19. Hiring sales people

Chapter 20. Managing sales people

Chapter 21. Conclusion

Introduction

So you're running a business or maybe you're thinking of setting up a new business. That makes you different to most people. It takes real guts, ambition and determination to set up and successfully run a business.

CONGRATULATIONS ON JOINING AN EXCLUSIVE CLUB.

Your business may be a brand new startup, it may have been running for a while, you might even have sales people working in your business. Many businesses start as the result of a spark of inspiration by the founder; an idea for a new product or a skill that they have that they think others might benefit from. Whatever your situation, and however groundbreaking your product or service may be, you need to be able to sell them to potential customers; if you don't sell, you don't make profits and without profits you quickly go out of business.

I've been selling and managing sales teams for far more years than I care to remember. It's what I do... it's what I enjoy. I get as much pleasure from helping sales people become successful as I ever did from closing sales, whether they were a few hundred pounds or over a million.

I've worked for, run and owned small businesses, so I understand the mind set it takes to be successful, I understand the pressure that business owners have to handle every day and I know how difficult it can be to find time to try and improve your skills.

I've sold products and services as varied as building materials, storage and logistics equipment, design services, telemarketing services, training services, IT systems management and testing software, satellite communications equipment and software and accounting and payroll software.

I've sold around the world from the UK to the USA, from Austria to Australia, from Italy to Indonesia, from Poland to Pakistan, from Sweden to Saudi Arabia, so I appreciate how important it is to understand local customs and culture.

I've experienced the highs and lows of selling; I always tell people who are new to selling that the highs you feel when you close that big deal, or that opportunity you've been working on for two years are the best you'll ever encounter in a working environment, and the lows when that big deal you thought was in the bag suddenly disappears or goes to a competitor, are the worst feelings in the world. If you can dust yourself off after losing a sale and start all over again, then you're part way to becoming successful.

When I started out on my sales career, finding new customers typically meant working through the Yellow Pages and Trade Directories and interminable cold calling. The world has changed, and now salespeople need to use a variety of methods to find and develop new sales prospects. We'll cover some of these later in the book.

I've read books that refer to "the art of selling". I don't believe that selling is an art; for me successful selling is a combination of a positive and determined mindset combined with a set of skills that can be learnt and polished over time.

This book is a summary of some of the skills I've learned over the course of my sales career. I hope that by reading it, you'll find a few ideas that will help you be more effective at selling,

Who Is This Book For?

This book isn't meant to be the ultimate sales guide for every type of business. If your business is in retail (both shops and online) or if your business provides commodity items (products where the customer knows exactly what they want and why they need it.. (think selling bricks to builders), then some of the topics we'll cover won't be particularly relevant.

If, on the other hand, you sell products or services to other businesses (B2B) and you're finding it difficult to identify and approach potential customers, or you're finding it difficult to explain your real value or differentiate yourself from your competitors, then read on.

If you're new to selling, or you've learned your selling skills by trying (and sometimes failing) and want to explore ways of improving your sales skills, then hopefully you'll find some new ideas and concepts that you can put into practice.

Whatever your reason for buying this book, (and thank you for doing so) take your time, think about the ideas and consider carefully how you can put them into use. With time and practice, you can improve your selling skills and by doing so, continue to grow your business.

HAPPY SELLING!

Chapter 1 - It's All About The Value

Traditional sales methodologies used to talk about selling based on features and benefits. Maybe you sell software to help customers quickly create invoices. It enables the user to quickly create attractive looking invoices which include a long list of products that they've sold along with the associated prices. They can even include their company logo on the invoice and edit the layout. These are the features. The benefits include the ability to quickly create an attractive looking invoice without having to look up a customer's address and automatically adding all the product prices, and calculating the totals and VAT.

However, when you buy anything, although it may have a practical use, it also has a value associated with it. When you buy a ready meal at the supermarket, you may be buying a food item that comes in easy to open packaging and has clear microwave cooking instructions prominently displayed. The real value, however, is that this food item will help you address your hunger, save valuable preparation time and ultimately help you survive (after all, we have to eat to stay alive).

We can take this idea further though. Imagine you go to a DIY store to buy a 7mm drill bit to put up some shelves. The feature is that the drill bit (used with a drill of course) provides the benefit of enabling you to create a hole in the wall, into which you can insert a wall fixing that will hold the shelf firmly to the wall. So maybe you could argue that when you're buying a drill bit, you're actually buying a hole. But why are you putting up a shelf in the first place? Maybe it's to hold that pile of books that's been taking up space in the corner of your living room ever since you moved into the house. So you could actually argue that the real value of the drill bit is creating space in your living room!

Now, don't get me wrong, I'm not suggesting that when I go to buy a drill bit, I'm consciously thinking about all that lovely empty space I'm going to have once I've put the shelf up. Anyone who goes to buy a drill bit almost certainly knows what it does, how to use it and why they need it, and this is pretty much the norm when it comes to anything you buy in a retail environment, whether that's in store or online.... the need has already been recognised, the decision to buy has already been made, and the only question is which particular drill bit you're going to choose from the available selection.

In a Business to Business (B2B) environment however, it's not always as simple as this. Unless you're selling a commodity item where the reasons to buy and the benefits are already known and understood, then quite often the potential customer may not even be aware of the value that your product offers to them, or even that it exists!

Being able to clearly communicate the real commercial value of your products or services is the key to getting potential customers to consider buying from you.

Let's go back to our invoicing software. Your potential customer may be quite happy creating invoices in an Excel template, typing in the customer name and address, manually adding the products and prices, calculating the total value of all the products sold, the VAT and the invoice total, printing the invoice, filing a copy, and mailing the invoice to the customer. After all, that's the way they've always done it... and it works. So when you tell them you've got this amazing piece of software that makes invoicing easy and only costs £20 per month, it's hardly surprising that they won't buy it. They're happy with the way that they're working at the moment and they don't think that they can justify the extra £20 per month.

But how long does all this take if they're raising several invoices a day? Let's assume that they spend an hour and a half every day raising and sending invoices and that by using your invoicing software, this would only take half an hour a day.

Maybe the potential customer's profits are falling and they're worried about being able to pay their staff. They know that this is a problem, but they're struggling to find ways to sort it.

If they spent an extra hour selling each day, maybe they could sell another £500 worth of products. So in a month, by using your software, they could save 20 hours of time to spend selling (1 hour per day x 5 days x 4 weeks). That's £10,000 of extra sales revenue that they can generate every month and it will only cost them £20. Let's assume they make a 25% gross profit on every sale. In a year, they'll have generated £120,000 of extra sales revenue and £30,000 extra profit, at an additional cost of £240 ! Now they've got their profit back on track, staff are being paid and the pressure's off.

That's a pretty compelling sales message. Now, when they say they can't afford the £20 subscription cost per month, you can highlight that it could help them make £30,000 extra profit (provided they actually use the extra time to sell!).

Chapter 2 - So Where Do We Start?

The first stage of developing a really compelling sales message (or sales narrative) is to work out the true commercial value of your product or service.

Think about your own business and your customers' businesses; what are the major business problems that they might be facing? What is it that they constantly worry about? It might include:

- Static or falling revenue
- Static or falling profits
- Restricted or declining cash flow
- Inability to pay suppliers or worse still, staff
- Excess stock
- Slow moving stock
- Lack of time to grow the business
- Heavy admin workload
- Slow paying customers
- Underperforming staff
- Increasing raw material costs

I'm sure you can add many more to the list but this is a good starting point.

Now, think about the impact that these problems have on the business. What are the costs associated with these problems? Costs in this scenario could be quantitative such as monetary value, number of hours spent or wasted, or they could be qualitative such as poor product quality or damaged business reputation.

Let's look at the problem of falling profits. The impact on the business might be that the business can't afford to pay their suppliers or staff; it might even mean that they're having to seriously consider a redundancy programme. It might mean that they can't afford to buy that new machine they need to improve the quality of their current product which is damaging their reputation. It might mean that the business owner can't afford the extra payments they wanted to make into their pension plan.

The important thing to remember is that all perceived problems have an impact. One of our roles as sales people is to encourage the customer to open up, identify and acknowledge the problems that they're facing, and then work out what the impact of these problems may be, whether they're quantitative or qualitative.

We can take this a step further. Even businesses that appear successful might have greater ambitions. A business that is making £200,00 profit every year might be able to continue at this level quite happily, but if they actually want to increase this to £300,000 in order to pay bonuses to employees, increase pension contributions or buy new machinery to increase production capacity, then we can still categorise this as a "problem".

Exercise 1:

Draw up a list of business problems that potential customers might be facing and against each one, identify as many possible costs or impacts that these might have.

Business Problem	**Cost / impact of the Problem (Quantitative / Qualitative)**
Falling profits	Inability to pay suppliers
	Inability to pay staff
	Inability to buy new machinery
Restricted cash flow	Inability to buy more stock
	Inability to pay staff
Insufficient time for selling	Not meeting sales targets
	Not meeting profit targets
Customer complaints	Losing customers
	Losing sales revenue

You'll see that some of the entries in the "cost" column appear against more than one "Business Problem" entry. This is perfectly normal; it's potentially a good thing for you as it could mean that by helping the customer to address one problem, you'll actually be helping them to address other problems as well.

Now we have our list of business problems and their possible impacts, we can start to think about how your product or service helps address these issues.

Let's go back to the example of selling invoicing software. We've identified that our potential customer is experiencing falling profits, and they're worried abut being able to pay their staff, so redundancies might be on the cards. We've also identified that they don't have time to focus on more sales activity, they can't afford to employ a full time sale person and that they're creating their invoices in Excel.

Now we're in the position of being able to explain that by using our software, we can help them free up 20 hours of extra time for selling each month, which could help address the issue of falling profits

Exercise 2:

Add an extra column to our table of Business problems and costs, this one explaining how you help address the cost or impact of the problem.

Business Problem	Cost of the Problem (Quantitative / Qualitative)	How we help address the problem
Falling profits	Inability to pay suppliers	Freeing up 20 hours / month to spend selling, generating £30k profit
	Inability to pay staff	Freeing up 20 hours / month to spend selling, generating £30k profit
	Inability to buy new production equipment	Freeing up 20 hours / month to spend selling, generating £30k profit

Restricted cash flow	Inability to buy more stock	Freeing up 20 hours / month to spend selling, generating £30k profit
	Inability to pay staff	Freeing up 20 hours / month to spend selling, generating £30k profit
Insufficient time for selling	Not meeting sales targets	Freeing up 20 hours / month to spend selling, generating £30k profit
	Not meeting profit targets	Freeing up 20 hours / month to spend selling generating £120k sales
Customer complaints	Losing customers	Eliminate invoicing errors and complaints & retain customers
	Losing sales revenue	Eliminate invoicing errors and retain sales revenue

So now we have a clearer understanding of the types of business problems that our potential customers might be facing, the impact that having these problems might have on the customer and an explanation of how our product service could help the customer solve the problem.

THAT'S THE REAL VALUE OF YOUR PRODUCT OR SERVICE!

Chapter 3 - Who Should We Be Selling To?

It never ceases to amaze me how many business owners that I talk to who, when asked the question, "who is your ideal customer?", they answer "anyone who will buy our product".

In a sense that's true, but if you don't know anything about the characteristics of an ideal customer, you're going to have to talk to a huge number of businesses before you find one you can actually help.

If you're selling car repair services, there's no point promoting your services to someone who doesn't own a car.

Think about your existing customers. What are the common business problems they face that you identified in Exercise 1? What other characteristics do they have common in common? Do they operate within specific markets, do they make similar products, are they in specific geographical areas, are they a particular size? (sales revenue, profit, number of employees, number of locations etc). Do they have a particular marketing budget? Do they use particular types of technology? How long have they been around? Are they a startup or an established business? Do they have common reporting structures or departments? Do they sell to similar types of customers? Are there any "red flags" you find with prospects who never buy? (Prospects in particular countries, markets, or technology users).

If we go back to our example of a business selling simple invoicing software, we can make some reasonable assumptions about the type of business that **wouldn't** be interested in our product. A business with sales of £20m will likely already have sophisticated invoicing and accounting software in place, whereas a business with sales of £100,000 might not. A business that sells it's products around the world would need to be able to manage international tax rules, whereas a business that only sells to customers in the UK will only need to manage VAT.

Now we can start to develop a set of characteristics that an "ideal" customer might have. For our invoicing software provider, we might say that an ideal customer has sales revenues below £100,000, less than 5 employees, sells a large range of products and only sells in the UK. By defining what an ideal potential customer looks like, we can start to focus our selling activities on businesses that match this profile, and avoid wasting huge amounts of time and effort.

Exercise 3:

Draw up a list of characteristics that would apply to an "ideal customer".

You could consider aspects such as

- Business size
- Maturity of business (startup, established etc)
- Location
- Number of employees
- Products / Services sold
- Number of physical locations
- Market sectors served
- Geographical markets served
- Technology used

It's also important to think about the roles of individuals within a potential customer and how the business problems we've defined affect them as individuals. Take the example of a business that makes machinery for printing and binding books. Logically, you might think that you should be talking to the Manufacturing Director who will be interested in anything that speeds up production, reduces errors, minimises down time and increases quality. But the Financial Director will be interested in anything that helps improve revenue, profit or cash flow. The Sales Director might be interested in ensuring high quality and keeping prices as low as possible. The HR Director might be interested in machinery that reduces the number of industrial accidents. The Managing Director is likely to be interested in solutions to any major problem within the business.

If we've been able to identify the problems that each of these individuals want to address and can clearly demonstrate this to all of them, they are all more likely to support the decision to buy your machinery than if we'd only been talking to the Manufacturing Director.

What's critical here is that to effectively sell more complex products, you should be talking to more than one person within the customer's business. The subjects that you discuss with each individual may differ slightly, but the more ammunition you can gather to demonstrate how impressive your solution is to each of them, the more compelling the overall sales message will be.

It might be that for some prospects, talking to only one contact is all you need to do, but if your product is complex, sophisticated or wide reaching and your ideal customers usually have several job functions, then you may need to be talking to several people.

Exercise 4:

Think about all the various job titles and roles in your existing customers.

Who do you normally talk to?

Which other roles might be facing some of the business problems you've identified?

How does the way in which your product address these problems affect each individual?

Hopefully your business has spent a lot of time defining what makes it unique. It might be a unique product, your first class service, competitive pricing, or something else.

"Hopefully" is a big word..... it amazes me even now how often I ask the businesses I work with "Who is your ideal customer?" and the answer is, "Anyone who will buy from me!"

You may well have already experienced a bad customer. You invest huge amounts of your time working with them, provide the best service you can and yet despite all this, they're never happy. Not only is this demoralising for you and your staff, it's also costing you business time, money, resources and possibly damaging your reputation.

Customers that aren't a good fit cost money, time, and frustration.

Customers that are a good fit speed up the sales process, increase profits, and improve employee satisfaction.

The keys to finding the right customers is also knowing who not to sell to.

Once you've developed an ideal customer profile, it doesn't mean you can't say yes to customers outside of it or the profile can't develop as your business evolves.

BUT…. No One's Ideal Customer Is 'Everyone'

So once you're actually talking to potential customers, if you think that you genuinely can't help them, don't be afraid to walk away. A prospect won't blame you for concluding that you can't help them; they're more likely to be grateful and respect you for being honest with them.

Similarly, if you think that they're likely to be difficult to work with, then tread carefully. I worked with one customer once who bought some software from me. I had to work really hard to win the sale, but my determination to close the deal meant that I ignored some of the obvious warning signs. This particular customer turned out to be so demanding, so unreasonable and, at times, so downright rude, that we wasted days and days of time resolving perceived issues that really weren't important and my support team used to dread taking his calls. In the end, I politely advised him that we were no longer prepared to work with him and walked away. Needless to say, my support team were hugely grateful and it freed up more of my time to spend selling to customers who were a good fit.

Understanding which customers aren't a good fit for you is just as important as knowing which ones are. Get this right, and you'll avoid huge amounts of wasted time, wasted effort and personal frustration.

So now we understand the characteristics of our ideal potential customer, and we understand the job titles or roles within an ideal customer who we may be able to help. Now, instead of having to talk to hundreds of businesses to find one that might be interested in what we have to offer, we can immediately eliminate a large proportion of all businesses from our prospect list.

Imagine how much time you could save if instead of having to talk to a hundred businesses in order to make one sale, you only had to talk to ten businesses to make one sale. **You'd immediately save 90% of your selling time and still be generating the same results!**

Now consider what would happen if you still talked to a hundred prospects.... you'd actually end up selling to ten. **That's ten times the sales revenue for the same time and effort.**

You probably picked up this book, because you're concerned about how effective your selling activities are. Maybe your revenues are falling, maybe you're worried about how much profit you're making. By helping you to think of a set of characteristics that define who your ideal customer is, and by understanding how to communicate the value of your product or service, and which roles within the customer you should be presenting this value to, I've just enabled you to save 90% of your selling time, or generate ten times the revenue.

That's the real value of this book (see what I did there?)

REMEMBER - No One's Ideal Customer Is Everyone.

Chapter 4 - The Competition

B2B sales is highly competitive. Whatever it is that you sell, there'll be some form of competition, even if it's just "doing nothing". Competition will almost always raise its head at some point in the selling process. It might be at the beginning, it might be half way through, or it might not appear until the very end. Like it or not, there's always a competitor or an alternative option waiting to derail your well planned and executed sales strategy.

So how do you know when and how to sell over your competitors? Who are they? When should you begin to discuss them? How do you bring them into the conversation? What do you say about them?

Surprisingly, if you've thought in advance how to approach the topic of competition, it can even be to your advantage, especially if you can anticipate competition related objections that potential customers might raise. Here are a few tips to consider when working out how to address the topic.

Never talk down your competitors

Irrespective of whether you're selling to other small businesses or larger enterprises, be humble. Humility shows that you really care and have empathy with your prospect. If you talk badly about your competitors at any point you're showing anything but humility. You also risk losing that credibility you've worked so hard to create. It's always best to show respect to everyone in your marketplace.

Know your competition inside and out

You have to be confident in your own product and service.... that goes without saying. But it's equally important to really understand your competitors' products and services. This will give you the confidence to talk about the key differences between your product and those of the competition. If you know your market better than anyone else, it will give you a competitive advantage.

Companies that really don't understand their competitive advantage will make statements like "Our product is better quality" or "Our service is better." Even if a company has better quality or better service, it's unlikely to convince a customer just by saying so, because many of its competitors will be saying the exact same thing! You have to define quality or show how your service differs from the competition.

Review everything that you offer... product features, company strengths, support services, value-added benefits, etc.

Rank each element of your offering (e.g. definite disadvantage, slight disadvantage, seems equal, slight advantage, definite advantage) against the competition.

Most importantly, identify your relative strengths and weaknesses.

Ranking each element of your offering compared to your competitors enables you to clearly communicate your strengths and allows you describe what those differences are. It enables you to compare each component of your complete solution (not just the product itself), and then highlight your advantages and disadvantages. Sometimes, the total impact of all the benefits is more significant than any one feature, and the total offering provides the comparison. (In other words, the whole may be greater than the sum of its parts).

Each comparison will differ based on the buyer's priorities, who your competitors are, and which products or services you are selling. A comprehensive competitive analysis will serve as a good starting point for presenting the information to the buyer in the most effective way.

Always be tactful in your approach

Before you can address a competitive threat, you need to know which competitive options your prospect is considering, and the earlier you can find this out, the better. The point at which it's appropriate to mention competitive options really depends on the situation and the type of sale, and where your prospect is in the buying cycle. An inbound sales enquiry prospect will be different to an outbound sales prospect.

With inbound enquiries, the prospect is much more likely to be closer to buying because they'll almost certainly have already done some research into possible solutions to their problems. In situations like these, you can justifiably ask earlier. Always be tactful when you do decide to ask. There are a few ways to do this but my preferred option is to do it once you're comfortable that you've built a strong rapport with your prospect.

Try asking… "What do you really like about other providers you have seen?" This gives you the opportunity to find out which competitors you're up against without directly asking. Once you know which options are being considered you can ask what's missing from them, or you could ask what else the prospect would like to see. This approach gives you real clues as to which competitor you're up against, along with information about deficiencies that you may be able to exploit.

With outbound opportunities (sales opportunities that you have developed from scratch) if you can avoid specifically talking about competition, then do it. If you think your prospect hasn't even considered looking at other solutions, try asking "have you done anything about this yet?" or "how far have you got with this?"

Differentiate yourself

Once you know what the possible competitive deficiencies are, put yourself in your competitors' shoes. Based on your competitive research, think about how they sell their product, how they communicate the value they offer, and what unique selling propositions (USP's) they highlight. Once you understand this, you can identify their strengths and weaknesses so you know which of your own strengths you can emphasise. Try to do this in a subtle way. Clearly focusing on the differences, without actually mentioning the competitor by name, is just as effective. For example, if you offer really impressive support services to your customers, but you believe that your competition is more "hands off", then talking about the importance of high quality support during your discussion will give you a real edge.

Give yourself the advantage

During the sales process, to maximise the likelihood that you'll win, you need to be sure that you've covered every possible angle. Think about developing a product comparison document that you can share with prospects which will encourage them to compare your product with those of your competitors. This is where really understanding the value that you provide comes into it's own; if you understand your own value in detail, you can make a big play about those areas where you're different. Concentrate on your strengths. Make sure your customer understands exactly why you think your product or service is better and what that means in terms of the value it will give to them. Don't worry too much about what you can't do, instead concentrate on what you can do and the value that this delivers to your customer. Sell your strengths.

Chapter 5 - How Do Customers Buy?

Now we understand the real value of our product, it's useful to understand how businesses actually go about buying products or services.

People buy in different ways; some buyers know what they need, why they need it, when they need it and how much they're prepared to pay for it. I call these prospects "Educated Buyers".

Others don't even realise that they have a problem that your product or service could address, but once you've been able help them understand the problems they're facing and have precisely explained the real value of your product, then..... and only then, will they buy. I call these prospects "Uneducated Buyers".

The way you communicate your products to potential customers subtly varies depending on whether your potential buyer is an educated buyer or an uneducated buyer.

Let's consider our invoicing software business.

An educated buyer has decided that they want to buy invoicing software. Now they need to find a potential supplier of software that enables them to quickly create good looking invoices. For a buyer like this, the information you provide to them simply needs to explain that you provide an invoicing software. Or does it?

If that's the only information you provide on your web site, then they might well find you through an internet search, but they'll also find every other supplier of invoicing software that does the same thing. They'll check out each supplier's website, maybe take out a free trial and perhaps talk to the supplier. From the selection of products that gives them what they believe they need, more often than not, they'll buy the cheapest. So how do you help them decide that your software is better than the rest? It comes back to communicating the value. The prospect has done an internet search, found your product and sees that it meets their "requirements". At this stage, if you're able to explain how, by using your software, not only will they meet the need they'd already identified, you'll also be providing more value to them than they'd originally expected, then they are more likely to buy your product, and they may well be prepared to pay a higher price than your competition offers. This is why explaining the business value of your products or services on your website is absolutely crucial. Simply listing a set of features and benefits won't necessarily educate a potential buyer about the full value they could derive from using your product.

To find educated buyers, we need to communicate the business value of our products in places where potential customers will be looking. The obvious place for this is your web site, but we'll look at other options later.

Now that's all well and good for educated buyers, but uneducated buyers don't realise that they have a problem that you can solve, so they won't be looking for a solution, they won't be running an internet search and they won't see your web site. To get their attention, we need to encourage them to start thinking about the problems that they might be facing and explain how we address them. Once they see this message, then it's more likely that it will trigger the idea that they should perhaps be talking to you.

So how do we get our value proposition across to potential customers who don't even realise that they have a problem you can solve?

When I started my career, the internet and web sites didn't exist (yes, I really am that old!), Marketing and Sales were thought of as entirely different functions within a business.

Marketing Departments were full of creative types, tasked with generating incoming sales leads through advertising and attendance at Trade Shows.

Sales Departments were full of driven, money motivated types who expected Marketing to provide leads for them to go and convert into sales. If the Sales Department did any of their own lead generation, it typically involved trawling through the Yellow Pages (remember them?) or huge Trade Directories to find companies to cold call. One company I worked for sold storage and distribution equipment that was used in warehouses and on lorries. When I was out visiting potential customers, typically located on industrial estates, I'd inevitably drive past other businesses with large warehouses and fleets of lorries, so I'd call in at reception, ask for a compliment slip and the name of the warehousing or distribution manager so that I could call them on my next day in the office.

Guess what?….. The world has changed. Nowadays the cross over between Marketing and Sales has become so large, it's almost impossible to tell where one ends and the other begins. The important factor to bear in mind is that Marketing and Sales activities need to be completely aligned. Once you've defined the value that you offer, then every single method you use to you communicate that value to potential customers, whether that's on your web site, at trade shows, on internet forums, in phone calls, emails and physical sales visits needs to be telling the same story.

I often read articles that say things like "cold calling is dead". I'm not sure I entirely agree with this, but it's certainly nowhere near as effective as it used to be. When was the last time you received a call from someone offering you PPI refunds or offering help in connection with a recent card accident you were involved in? How did you react?

I know how I react! I tell them to take my name off their list and end the call immediately. But why do I react this way?

Firstly, it's because neither service is of interest to me. I didn't have PPI and I haven't had a motoring accident in years (famous last words!).

Secondly, it's because the phone call is typically impersonal; I'd almost guarantee that the caller is using a script that they've been told to use. Years ago (here comes the reference to my age again), I would regularly get phone calls from Double Glazing companies. It was obvious from the outset that the caller was using a script, telling me that they offer fantastic quality doors, windows and conservatories and how they have a special offer for new customers this month and when would be a good time for one of their representatives to visit me to provide a quote. I used to play a game with them; I'd start asking random questions whilst they were talking. "Do you do them in blue?" "How about round windows?" More often than not, the caller would be completely thrown; their sole responsibility was making the call and making an appointment. They didn't know enough about their products to be able to answer my questions. All they knew was the script. And even when I bought a brand new house with double glazing already fitted, I'd still get these calls. It's no wonder that their conversion rate of calls to appointments would be so low.

Clearly, these companies hadn't attempted to work out who their ideal customer was..... someone who lives in a brand new house that already has double glazing isn't a potential customer. So why bother calling them in the first place?

To find new customers, your business, and your sales people need to be visible in places where potential customers might be. If a potential customer doesn't know that you even exist, or if they don't realise that you might be able to help them solve a problem, then you'll never get to talk to them. Yes, you need to have a website, but you also need to be visible and active elsewhere; on social media, on internet forums and web sites that are relevant to your potential customers, and at Trade Shows or events your potential customers might visit.

The Power of Social Media

Do you have a LinkedIn account? If not, you should have! LinkedIn is one of the most effective means of finding potential customers. You can search for individual people, you can search for individual companies and see who works for them, you can search for specific job titles, you can search for specific terms that may be relevant to the type of business you want to approach.... LinkedIn is the world's biggest Trade Directory. Once you've found potential customers and contacts, you can connect with them so that they see information that you post on the site, you can send them direct messages even if you don't have an email address or phone number for them. The more people you connect with, the bigger your potential network of contacts become.... so start connecting. Right now!

So you've connected with someone you think might be in need of your product. Now what? Yes, you could send them a direct message, and you might get a response, but put yourself in their shoes. You've just received a request from someone you don't know to connect on LinkedIn, and once you've accepted the connection request, the first thing you receive from them is a sales pitch. It's all a bit cold and impersonal isn't it? I know lots of people who, if they receive an approach like this, a) don't reply and b) delete the connection. If this happens, you've lost a potentially valuable connection and even if at some point in the future they identify a potential requirement for your product, you've already soured the relationship.

What's much more effective is a softer approach; an approach that gets them thinking about issues they hadn't previously considered, an approach that starts to educate them about how you might be able to help them without ramming your products down their throat. Some of the ways you can do this include:

- Posting articles or case studies about how your customers have solved specific business problems with your help.

- Posting articles about topics that are of general interest within your target market

- Posting news stories about new customers you've converted or awards that you've won.

- Sharing and commenting on postings that your potential customers have made. This shows that you're interested in what they have to say and that you're someone with opinions and insights that might be valuable to them.

Using LinkedIn in this way helps you start to build a relationship with potential customers; a relationship that's based on mutual respect and trust, a relationship that means that they may just contact you directly to understand more about how you can help them, or at least may be open to you making a direct approach at a later time.

All of this takes time, it takes persistence, and it means you have to put effort into making regular postings and monitoring, commenting on and sharing postings that your prospects are making. Over time, you'll start to build a loyal following who might just engage with you and even share the postings that you've made, which will make you visible to other potential customers that you're not yet connected to.

You can take the same approach with other social media platforms like Twitter, Instagram and Facebook. the platforms you use will depend on which are the most relevant to the type of organisation and individual that you ideally want to talk to. So do your research.. what do your existing customers do, which platforms do they use, how do they use them?

Online Forums & Special Interest Websites

Is there a news and information web site that caters specifically for the type of business that you sell to? If there is, these can be an absolute goldmine of information; everything from industry insights that you can use to generate your own articles and postings on Social Media, identifying contacts who you can start to connect with on LinkedIn, and other companies who also sell to your target market where, perhaps, there's an opportunity for you to work with them, recommending each other's products.

Most of these types of forums will offer opportunities for businesses to advertise or post articles (usually for a fee), providing a means of promoting your company name to a wide audience.

Using Referrals

Your existing customers are arguably your best source of high quality, new sales leads. If your customers are happy with your products or services, if they understand the value that you've delivered, then they may well mention you favourably to other businesses that they know and work with. Ask your existing customers if they know of any other businesses who might benefit from working with you, and if they do, better still ask them to make an introduction for you. At the very least, calling or emailing a prospect and being able to say, "John Smith at ABC Ltd suggested that I get in touch because he thought I may be able to help you" is far more personal and effective than a cold call or email, because you're starting from a position of credibility. If your customer actually makes an introduction, then the door is already firmly open for you.

Case Studies

I mentioned posting case studies on Social Media earlier, and here's why. Like referrals, case studies which explain why an existing customer uses your products and the value that they've generated from it is an incredibly powerful way of communicating your value; it gives you instant, proven credibility in the eyes of the reader.

Thought Leadership

We've already talked about making you and your company visible on Social media. Some of the most successful people I know do this on a regular basis. The articles they post may not even directly relate to the products and services they provide, but the mere fact that potential customers can see that they have valuable knowledge about the industry in which they work, builds a picture that they are experts in their field, and again, this all helps build credibility and trust within the audience.

Trade Shows

I have really mixed views on Trade shows / exhibitions; they can be good, but they can also be a huge waste of time and money. Obviously, the best ones are those that attract large numbers of visitors who potentially have an interest in your product. They provide an opportunity for you to connect with large numbers of potential customers, perhaps provide product demonstrations, and they also help you build your brand awareness; or put more simply, "get your name out there".

Most larger Trade Shows provide a variety of different exhibitor options, from a small space with walls on two or three sides (commonly referred to as a shell scheme) where you simply turn up and use a Pop Up stand, all the way through to options where you pay for an area of floor space and then work with a specialist exhibition stand designer who will design a stand for you, build it and remove it at the end of the exhibition. Shell scheme options can cost as little as a few hundred pounds, space only design and build options can run into the tens or even hundreds of thousands of pounds.

Deciding which option is best for you very much depends on how much you can afford to spend and what your objectives are for attending the event. I've worked for companies in the past who's sole objective for exhibiting at an event was to promote their company and keep their name visible to existing customers who expected to see them at the event. They weren't especially worried about whether or not it directly generated new business for them, but for most small businesses, this is an expensive way of promoting their brand. If, on the other hand, you believe that the cost of attending (including the exhibition space, any marketing material you decide to give away, your stand (whether designed or Pop Up), travel to and from the event, and the time of your staff) is less than the amount of new business you can generate as a direct result of attending, then it's worth considering.

Most Exhibition Organisers should be able to give you an idea of the number of visitors that they're expecting, especially if the event has been run previously, and they'll probably be able to give you a break down of the visitors in terms of industries or job roles. Treat this information with caution though. One company I worked for exhibited at a new Trade Show who advertised that they were expecting around 2,000 visitors. Once we got to the venue, however, it became clear that the organisers were actually running three events side by side, none of which were related. Not only was the estimate of 2,000 visitors overly optimistic, it also related to the total of all three events, not the specific event we were exhibiting at. The overall experience wasn't good and the amount of business generated as a result of exhibiting didn't come close to covering the cost of attending. Needless to say, we didn't go back the following year.

Networking Events

You've probably seen adverts for Business Networking Events; some run by local organisations, others are part of national networking organisations. Typically, they provide an opportunity for each attendee to provide a short "pitch" about what they do and what they offer, followed by an opportunity to talk to the other attendees in an informal environment.

Small business networking events, just like exhibitions can be useful, but they can also be a complete waste of time and money. It very much depends on who's attending, and how relevant your products are to the other attendees. If you provide products or services that might be of interest to a wide range of companies (for example accountancy or legal services), then they can be worthwhile. If, on the other hand, your product is specific to a very targeted market (such as printing machinery or hazardous waste removal services), then they're probably worth giving a miss.

There is, however one other benefit that may be worth considering. If the attendees include organisations who wouldn't necessarily be interested in your products, but who also sell their products to the same type of customer as you, then there can be some value in building those relationships so that each of you can recommend each other's products when you're talking to potential customers.

Chapter 6 - Elevator pitches

Networking events or trade shows give you an opportunity to talk to potential customers, but typically, you don't have much time to explain what it is that you do and the value that you provide. That's where the concept of an "elevator pitch" comes in.

Imagine that you're visiting a big potential customer and on your way out, you find yourself in the lift (or elevator as our American cousins call them) with the CEO. This is your dream scenario to explain how you can help her; she's a captive audience for the two minutes it takes for the lift to get back to the ground floor. You open your mouth, and then pause. Where on earth do you start?

You try to organise your thoughts, but just as you're about to open your mouth to speak, the lift arrives at the ground floor and she's gone! You've lost the opportunity!

This is one situation where it helps to have an "elevator pitch." It's a short, pre-prepared explanation of what your organisation does, clearly and succinctly.

About the Technique

An elevator pitch is a brief, persuasive statement that you use to spark interest in what your organisation does. You can also use them to create interest in a project, idea, or product. A good elevator pitch should last no longer than a short ride in a lift.....maybe 20 to 30 seconds, hence the name.

They should be interesting, memorable, and to the point. They also need to explain what makes you – or your organisation, product, or idea – unique.

When to Use an Elevator Pitch

Using elevator pitches doesn't have to be restricted to sales situations. Of course you can use one to introduce your organisation to potential clients or customers, but you can also use them in your organisation to sell a new idea to a colleague, or to tell people about a change initiative that you're leading. You can even craft one to tell people what you do for a living. Their real value is in explaining a concept or idea quickly and effectively, and with real impact.

Creating an Elevator Pitch

It can take some time to get your pitch right. You'll likely go through several versions before finding one that is both compelling and sounds natural in conversation.

Follow these steps to create a great pitch, but bear in mind that you'll need to vary your approach depending on what your pitch is about.

1. Identify Your Goal

Start by thinking about the objective of your pitch. In a sales scenario, such as attending a networking event or Trade Show you're objective is tell potential clients about your organisation and trigger some interest.

2. Explain What You Do

Start your pitch by describing what your organisation does. Focus on the problems that you solve and how you help people. If you can, add information or a statistic that shows the value in what you do.

Ask yourself this question as you start writing: what do you want your audience to remember most about you?

Keep in mind that your pitch should excite you first; after all, if you don't get excited about what you're saying, neither will your audience. People may not remember everything that you say, but they're likely to remember your enthusiasm.

Let's create an elevator pitch for our business selling invoicing software that describes what the company does. We could say, "My company provides invoicing software for small businesses." Not particularly inspiring or memorable is it?

A better explanation would be, "My company provides software that enables businesses to quickly generate invoices. This saves them time and reduces the risk of making errors in their invoices". That's much more interesting, and shows some of the value that we provide to our customers, but maybe we can make it even more compelling.

3. Explain the real value

Think back to Chapter 2 when we looked at the commercial value that we provided by solving the business problems that our potential customers might be facing. We identified that some customers could save significant amounts of administration time which could now be used to generate extra sales revenue, and by eliminating invoicing errors, we could avoid losing loyal customers and retain the sales revenue that we generated from them. And if we have examples of exactly how much time customers have saved, how much more revenue they've been able to generate as a result, and the revenue they've retained by not losing customers, then our proposition becomes really compelling.

4. Put It All Together

When you've completed each section of your pitch, put it all together.

Then, read it aloud and use a stopwatch to time how long it takes. It should be no longer than 20-30 seconds. Otherwise, you risk losing the person's interest, or monopolising the conversation.

Then, try to cut out anything doesn't absolutely need to be there. Remember, your pitch needs to be snappy and compelling, so the shorter it is, the better!

Example:

Here's how your pitch could come together:

"My company provides software that enables businesses to quickly and accurately generate invoices. This saves them time and reduces the risk of making errors on their invoices. Some of our customers have been able to use this time to increase sales by 20% and increase customer loyalty by 30%"

Short, to the point and compelling!

It's worth developing a number of elevator pitches that you can use depending on who you're talking to, what you know about their business, what business problems you think they may be facing and how you think you may be able to help them.

Exercise 5:

Write down three possible elevator pitches, making sure that they clearly and quickly explain what your business does, how this helps customers and the value that your product or service delivers.

5. Practice

Like anything else, practice makes perfect. Remember, how you say it is just as important as what you say. If you don't practice, it's likely that you'll talk too fast, sound unnatural, or forget important elements of your pitch.

Make sure you practice your elevator pitch regularly. The more you practice, the more natural it will become. You want it to sound like a smooth conversation, not an aggressive sales pitch.

Make sure that you're aware of your body language as you talk, as this conveys just as much information to the listener as your words do. Practice in front of a mirror or, better yet, in front of colleagues, friends or partners until the pitch feels natural. If you've never done this before it will feel really strange, if not embarrassing, but trying your pitch on people you know gives you the opportunity to make a complete mess of it, and refine it in a situation where it really doesn't matter. Far better to make a mess of it with friends, than in front of a potential customer.

As you get used to delivering your pitch, it's a good idea to vary it a little – the idea is that it doesn't sound too formulaic or like it's pre-prepared, even though it actually is!

Remember to tailor your pitch for different audiences. If appropriate, you can develop a number of elevator pitches that cater for different audiences.

Chapter 7 - Starting To Sell

So now we've defined what our real value is to potential customers, we've defined what an ideal customer looks like, we've identified the job roles within those business that we think might be most interested in our products, we've started to build our network of contacts though Social Media, we've been posting articles, commenting on and sharing their content and we've begun to demonstrate that we're thought leaders in our particular field, and we've built up some credibility in our market, we can start directly approaching potential customers.

Maybe you could start by picking up the phone and calling a prospect, maybe you could send an email, maybe you could send a message via LinkedIn. But how do you start the communication?

"But".. I hear you ask.. "didn't you say that cold calling wasn't particularly effective?" You're right… I did. But what we're talking about here isn't "cold", because you're approaching potential customers with whom you've already built a relationship on LinkedIn, Twitter or you've met them at a trade show or networking event.

The first direct communication, whether it's by phone, email or LinkedIn message needs to demonstrate some real value to whoever you're approaching. Nowadays there's an assumption that this first approach will be by telephone or online in some way. But don't discount printed letters. When I started my career, emails didn't exist, so the phone and physical mail were the two options I had for contacting potential customers. Over time, people became fed up with the amount of sales related mail they were receiving and it became less and less effective. Now the opposite is potentially true. Receiving a printed and personalised letter is almost a rarity, and may help you get the attention of a potential customer. Try it..... you may be surprised at the results.

The key with making this first contact is not to make it sound like a cold call. There are a number of ways you can achieve this. Here are some ideas.

Ask A Question Relating To Your Business Value

Hi Carol,

I've got a question for a fellow business owner - how do you find enough time to spend on selling your products?

The reason why I'm asking this is because we have a software product that helps our customers free up hours of time every week that they can now use to sell more.

Would you or somebody from your team be able to spend 15 minutes this week to take a quick look?

Reference An Article Or Posting Of Theirs That You've Seen

Hi David,

I really enjoyed your article on LinkedIn about how difficult it is to get new visitors to come to your web site when you're new to the market.

Many of our clients used to have the same problem, but have been able to increase web site traffic by 30% since they started using our services.

Would you be interested in a quick phone call to see if we might be able to help you?

If your first contact is made by phone, ask if they have 15 minutes now to see if you can help them. If the answer's no, try and schedule a better time to call back.

Reference A News Story On Their web Site

Hi Angela

Congratulations on being awarded the contract to print this year's HMRC Tax Guide. It sounds like a huge opportunity for you, but I'm sure it also raises some challenges.

Some of the largest UK Printing Companies use our industrial printers because they speed up production, reduce errors, minimise down time and increase quality.

Could you spare 15 minutes to explore whether this might help you grow your business further?

Again, if your first contact is made by phone, ask if they have 15 minutes now to see if you can help them. If the answer's no, try and schedule a better time to call back.

In all three examples, there are a number of aspects that are really important to note:

1. The messages are all personalised to the reader (relating to their role, referencing an article they've written or mentioning recent news story about their business). They're absolutely NOT a generic sales message that might be sent to hundreds of business. Because they're personalised, the messages are appealing to the reader's personal situation or ego, which is much more likely to get their attention.
2. The messages all demonstrate some of the value that you offer. Given that we know why our potential ideal customers might be interested in our products, we can focus on one of the issues that we know we can address.
3. The messages have a "Call To Action" i.e. asking them to do something; in these examples this is a commitment of 15 minutes to take a look at our product or discuss it's relevance to them and their business. Using 15 minutes is quite deliberate; it's not much time, so it's not a big commitment. If there is real interest, it's easy enough to extend the resulting conversation or schedule more time with them at a later date.

4. The messages are short. They're all easy and quick to read, they don't go on and on about how long you've been in business, how many offices you have around the world, how many customers you have. They're to the point, demonstrate some potential value and ask the recipient to do something.

Include a relevant subject heading / email title with your message. You might try things like "Question for a fellow business owner", "Really enjoyed your article about xxxxx", or "Congratulations on the new contract". Like the message, the title is relevant to the recipient, it's not generic and it's to the point.

One other technique that can be quite powerful is to add a "PS' at the end of the message, such as a link to a relevant case study or article, maybe asking whether they'll be attending an event you're due to exhibit at soon, or mentioning the name of a mutual contact.

Make sure that you include your contact details in the message (Name, email address and phone number) and include a link to your website. This may sound blindingly obvious, but you'd be surprised as to how many messages I receive that don't have them included.

What if they don't respond?

Hopefully, your message will trigger a response. If it does.. great! Now you can make the first phone call or schedule a face to face meeting. We'll look at how to conduct these first conversations later.

But what if you don't get a response?

Over the years I've seen many sales people simply assume that if they don't get a response to an initial approach, then it means that the prospect isn't interested.... and just give up. But let's think about the prospect here; there could be any number of reasons why they haven't responded. Of course, a lack of interest might be one of them, but it could be that they're just really busy, maybe they might be interested, but they don't see it as a priority right now, maybe they've passed your message on to someone else, maybe they're on holiday or off sick. Only one of these reasons is actually an out and out rejection, the others could mean that there's some potential interest, so it's vital that we follow up on every single first message that we send.

When and how we follow up needs some thought. If you've sent me a message and I'm really busy and haven't got around to responding, and you keep calling me or emailing me every day for a week, I'm just going to get annoyed. If, on the other hand, I haven't responded because, whilst I'm possibly interested, I can't do anything with your information for another two months, and the next message you send me is in six month's time, then I'll probably forget about you or, worse still, buy someone else's product in two month's time.

It's all about finding a balance. Typically, I send follow up messages three to four days after the initial message. That's long enough for the recipient to have read the message, thought about it and made an initial evaluation of it's value, but short enough for them not have forgotten it.

The follow up, like the initial message, should be short and to the point. use something along the lines of "did you receive my message? Do you have 15 minutes to talk this week?" or " I wondered if you'd had a chance to read my message. Maybe we can schedule 15 minutes to talk?". Both of these are polite, non-aggressive and still include a "Call To Action".

Remember, there's a limit to how many follow up messages you should send. If you're too persistent, the recipient will just think you're hounding them and switch off. Two, possibly three follow up messages is what I recommend. If, after these you still haven't received any response, then it's unlikely that you're going to any time soon.

Rather than just walk away though, you can still leave the door open for a response later with a final, "last ditch" message. I use two variations on this approach. The first one goes along the lines of "I appreciate that this may not be of interest to you right now, but if the situation changes, please get in touch". This gives the recipient the option to talk to you when the time is right.

The second option goes along the lines of "I'm sure you don't want to keep receiving unwanted messages, so I'll assume that you're not interested in taking a look at our new product. If circumstances change in the future, then please get in contact."

This nicely draws a line under the communication, but leaves the door firmly open for them to get in touch if they want to. Having used this approach for several years, it still surprises me how many responses it actually triggers from contacts who start by apologising for not getting in touch, usually because they've just been busy. The point is, that you're being polite, recognising that the recipient might have other priorities right now, but still giving them an option to contact you if they want to.

And finally, if you've still not received any form of response, don't give up. Continue to comment on, or share their LinkedIn postings. It might trigger a response later or it might put your name in front on someone else who's a more likely prospect.

Chapter 8 - Making The First Call / Meeting

Hooray!! You've put time and effort into networking, putting case studies on your web site, making Social Media posts, connecting to potential customers on LinkedIn, commenting on and sharing their posts, sending initial LinkedIn messages or emails, attending Trade Shows, asking for referrals from existing customers and now a potential customer has responded and agreed to meet you or has scheduled a time for you to call.

Well done! That's real success and you deserve a hearty pat on the back.

Now what?

The process is exactly the same, irrespective of whether you've arranged a face to face meeting or a phone call. Let's look at an example.

Picture the scene.... Gavin is the man behind our invoicing software. He came up with the idea, wrote the first version of the software, uses the software in his own business and he's already got a hundred customers on board, most of whom found him via his website, took out a free trial and signed up without ever talking to him. Based on this success to date, he's absolutely convinced that he's got a winning formula. He wants to accelerate his sales, so he's been working through all the networking activity that we've just described. He's just had a response from Helen who runs a business that provides graphic design services to other small businesses. Most of her work is designing logos, business cards, promotional material for other small businesses.

Gavin dresses in his best suit, makes sure he's at Helen's office in plenty of time and gets shown into the meeting room.

“Good morning Helen, it’s a pleasure to meet you. Thanks for taking the time to meet me” says Gavin. “Thanks for coming in” says Helen. “I saw a couple of your LinkedIn posts and it got me thinking. I’ve been thinking about changing the way we create invoices for a while, so when I got your message, I took a look at your website and thought it might be useful to see if you can help us”.

“Great!” thinks Gavin. “She obviously needs invoicing software - This one’s in the bag already.” He opens up his laptop, turns to Helen and says “let me tell you a little about us and what we do, and show you the product”. Before Helen can reply, Gavin opens a PowerPoint presentation and proceeds to go through 48 slides that explain how long he’s been in business, how he created the product, how many people he has in his team, how he’s already got 100 customers using the software, how it works, how you set it up, how you use it and how wonderful his technical support is.

Next Gavin opens up the software, shows Helen how to create customer records, how to create products and prices, how to add her logo to the invoice layout, create an invoice and send it to a customer.

“So you can see how easy it is to use and how much time you’ll save by using it” says Gavin.

With a flourish he closes his laptop and says “And it only costs £20 per month! All you need to do is set up an account on our web site and you’ll be up and running in no time”.

Helen looks at him with a glazed look in her eye, pauses, then says “thanks for coming in Gavin. That’s been really useful and I can see how proud you are of your software. Let me think about it and I’ll get back to you”. She takes him back to reception, shakes his hand and says goodbye.

Gavin heads back to his office, feeling proud and absolutely convinced that by the time he gets there, Helen will have subscribed to the software on his web site.

Two days later, Gavin's sitting in his office. "That's strange" he thinks. "I was sure Helen would have signed up by now, but I can't see a new account yet". Frustrated, he picks up the phone and calls Helen. "Hi Helen. I noticed that you haven't set your account up yet. Is there a problem?".

"Thanks for calling Gavin" says Helen. "I thought long and hard about everything you showed me, but I've decided not to go ahead with your software. It's obviously good at what it does but I don't think it's right for my business. Thank you again for coming in to see me. Bye". The phone goes dead.

Gavin's devastated! "What went wrong?" he thinks. "I explained how established and successful we are and how the software works and how easy it is to use it. She told me she was thinking about changing the way she raises invoices. Why on earth doesn't she want to use it? What went wrong?"

If you've learned anything from this book so far, it should be pretty obvious what went wrong.

Did Gavin identify all (or even any) of the business problems that Helen is trying to fix? - No

Did he identify what the impact would be if Helen managed to fix these problems? - No

Did he explain how his software would help address these problems? - No

Did he make sure that Helen understood the real commercial value to her of using his software? - No

Gavin's approach is usually referred to as a "tell and sell" approach. It's all about the sales person. It doesn't in any way focus on the customer or the customer's situation, objectives, problems and needs. It doesn't tell a story that the prospect can empathise with. It doesn't demonstrate a clear link between the prospect's problems and the value they would obtain from using Gavin's software.

When anyone first starts selling, if they've not been given any sort of basic training, and especially if they're particularly excited and proud about what they're selling, then it's only natural that they want to tell people about it.

But effective selling is more about listening than it is about talking.

To be successful as sales people, we need to help potential customers understand and explain their business, define their objectives, understand their problems and their highlight their needs. Only when we've done this can we match up the needs with the value that we can provide. To do this well means asking lots of questions.

But therein lies a problem.

When I was little, my Mum taught me some really important life lessons. Some of these lessons kept me me safe, some helped me avoid getting into trouble at school, some stopped me embarrassing my parents in company.

This was all a very, very, very long time ago, but I still remember them, so clearly they made a strong impression.

How many of you remember your Mum telling you things like

"Don't talk to strangers"

"Don't interrupt"

"Stop asking questions"

"If you're asked a question… answer it"

These lessons are great… if you're a child….. but here's the news… they no longer apply now that you're an adult and especially if you're selling. The problem is that these lessons are so ingrained in our thinking that they affect how we behave in certain situations.

This is one of the reasons so many people struggle to sell.

Simple isn't it, but guess what?.... you're allowed to ignore your Mum (at least at work).

Selling involves talking to busy strangers, they'll ask you questions and you'll feel rude if you ask too many of your own. If you also add your pride, your ego and a fear of failure and you're almost certainly going to fail at prospecting, qualifying, negotiating and closing sales.

Changing ingrained belief systems is hard, especially those that you've had since childhood. And to change them you need to learn new techniques that result in different behaviour. Making the effort to regularly practice these new behaviours will enable you to change your inherent beliefs.

Sorry Mum x

Chapter 9 - SPIN® Selling

When a potential customer shows some interest in our products or services, whether that's by means of a direct, unprompted enquiry, or as a response to some earlier communication, then before we talk to them, preparation is absolutely essential. The more we know about the customer's business, the individuals that we're due to talk to and the possible issues they may be facing, the easier it is to guide the conversation to focus on them, and identify the ways we may be able to help them.

So how do we prepare?

The obvious starting point is to take a look at the customer's website. What do they do? What do they sell? Who do they sell it to? What problems do they solve for their customers? Is anything changing in their business? Are there any interesting news items? Have they won any big contracts or awards? Who are the key people within the organisation?

All of this information gives you an overview of their business and may well trigger some thoughts as to how you might want to position your product.

Next, take a look at the LinkedIn profile of the individual(s) you'll be talking to. What's their role and what are they responsible for doing? How long have they worked there? Have they made any interesting LinkedIn postings that relate to issues you may be able to solve?

Now we have an overview of the business and the individual, we need to think about how we're going to run the discussion. The more you prepare, the more likely it will be that you can control the direction of the discussion.... and the direction you want is to understand to what extent the customer has problems you can help solve, explain how you can help solve them and explain the commercial value that you provide. Do all of this and the customer is more likely to want to go ahead and buy from you.

Bear in mind, however, that there may also be instances where you identify that you really can't help a potential customer. If you do, never try and convince them to buy.... honesty is always the best option. They'll respect you for being honest and if their business changes in the future in a way that means you could help, they're more likely to come back to you. They may even refer you to another business who you can actually help.

When we looked at our business value in Chapter 2, we identified some of the business problems that potential customers may be facing and how we help solve these problems.

First we should draw up a list of questions that will help us understand more precisely what these problems are and what value we can provide. These questions can cover a range of aspects, so putting some structure around our questions will help us control the direction of the discussion.

I've read more books about selling skills than I care to remember, but there's one in particular that resonated with me because the structure and process it recommends is simple, logical and easy to understand.

If you want to explore more, take a look at "SPIN® Selling" by Neil Rackham and for some really practical exercises to help you put SPIN® Selling into practice, look at "The SPIN® Selling Fieldbook".

Some people might criticise me for recommending someone else's sales methodology rather than developing my own, but I do it for good reasons... SPIN® Selling is based on a huge amount of research into sales techniques, looking at what works, and what doesn't. More than that, it's been proven to be successful time and time again, so what's the point in reinventing a fully functioning wheel?

Neil breaks down the sales process into four distinct stages:

Opening - getting the discussion started and positioning yourself to ask questions.

I**nvestigating** - Asking questions and understanding the buyer's needs and concerns

Demonstrating Capability - Showing how you can help

Obtaining Commitment - Gaining agreement to the next step.

Think back to Gavin's meeting with Helen; how much of the process did he actually follow?

He opened the discussion but he didn't make any attempt to position himself to ask questions.

Did he investigate the buyer's needs and concerns? - Absolutely not!

Did he demonstrate his ability to help? Well, yes, but only his ability to help solve the problems he **assumed** Helen had.

Did he obtain commitment to move to the next step? - Absolutely not!

Opening the discussion simply means explaining who you are and why you're there, (but **NOT** giving any details of your product or service) and getting the buyer's consent for you to ask questions about their business.

So Gavin might have said.. "Good morning Helen. Thanks for getting in contact. You mentioned that you'd been thinking about changing the way you handle invoicing, so I'd like to understand more about your thinking and see if we can help. Is that OK?"

Notice that in this example, Gavin hasn't mentioned anything about his product, he hasn't tried to solve any problems; all he's done is introduced himself, set the scene, put Helen at ease and asked for permission to continue.

Helen is almost certainly going to agree to this approach, which allows Gavin to start asking questions. And this is where the SPIN® Selling model comes in to play.

SPIN® Selling breaks down the investigation process into four discount elements:

S - Situation questions that help us understand the current status of the customer's business. During this stage we can explore what's happening within the business, what they sell, who they sell to, how the business is doing etc.

P - Problem questions that identify specific problems that the customer is facing right now.

I - Implication questions that help us understand the impact that these problems are having on the business.

N - Need Payoff questions that clarify the value, importance or usefulness of a solution to the buyer's problem.

Let's start with Situation questions. In Chapter 2, we thought about some of the possible business problems that customers might be facing, such as static revenue, falling profits, cash flow problems etc. Our Situation questions need to be very high level and relate to the current status of the business. At this stage, don't specify any of the possible problems we have in mind (and that we can solve)… we're just getting the customer to set the scene.

Exercise 6:

Think about the examples of Situation questions that you could use to start a discussion with the customer.

Situation Questions
Q1. How is business right now?
Q2. How many invoices do you raise each month?
Q3. Are you meeting your sales revenue targets?
Q4.
Q5.

Continue adding as many questions as you can come up with, but try not to ask too many situation questions. Keep them focussed on topics that might enable you to uncover problems later in the discussion.

Once we have a high level understanding of the current status of the customer's business, we can move to Problem Questions. Problem questions focus on difficulties or dissatisfactions that the buyer is experiencing with the existing situation.

Exercise 7:

Think about Problem Questions you can ask to uncover real problems that the customer is currently facing.

Problem Questions
Q1. How long does it take you to raise invoices every month?
Q2. How many mistakes appear on invoices because of incorrect product descriptions or prices?

Q3.
Q4.

Again, add as many Problem questions as you can think of. Now we understand the specific problems the customer is facing, we can explore the impact of these problems on the business.

Exercise 8:

Think about Implication questions you could ask that quantify the impact of problem the customer faces. Impact questions are incredibly important, because they help the buyer focus on the true cost of the problems on the business.

Impact Questions
Q1. How do you feel about the amount of time you currently spend raising invoices?
Q2. How do customers react when they find errors on your invoices?
Q3.
Q4.

Now we understand the implication of the problems the buyer faces, we can help them clarify **and confirm** specific needs that they have. Implication questions ask about the value or usefulness of a potential solution. Getting the buyer to confirm these needs is much more powerful than us simply assuming that we understand their needs… now we're working to their agenda.

Exercise 9:

Think about Need Payoff questions you could use to help clarify the value that the customer would receive by solving the problems you;ve identified.

Need Payoff Questions
Q1. How else could you use the time you currently spend raising invoices?
Q2. If you eliminated errors on invoices, how many customers would you avoid losing?
Q3. If you could spend an extra hour every day selling, how much more revenue could you generate?
Q4.
Q5.

So now we've explored the customer's current situation, we've managed to get the customer to highlight problems that they face, they've described the implication to the business of these problems, and we've got them to confirm specific needs that they have that, if solved, will enable them to generate a real business benefit.

At this stage, it's important to summarise what you've uncovered and get the customer to agree that your understanding is correct.

"OK Helen. It seems that you're spending around an hour and a half every day raising invoices, and that customers regularly report errors with product descriptions and prices on invoices that you send out. If you could reduce the amount of time spent on raising invoices and correcting errors, you could spend this time selling to more customers, and this could potentially generate an extra £30,000 of profit each year. If you could stop the invoicing errors, you'd eliminate customer complaints and avoid losing customers. Is this correct?"

Put yourself in the buyer's shoes..... are they really going to say no to a summary like that?!! And the more we can get a potential buyer to say "yes", the easier it becomes to lead them along the path to saying yes to a sale.

No we've helped the customer to agree that they have problems that they need to fix, and they've understood the business benefits of fixing them. Now, and only now, can we explain how we can help solve the problems. In Gavin's case, now would be the right time to demonstrate his software. In your business, maybe a product demonstration is appropriate, but maybe an explanation of your services, or a relevant customer case study would be a more effective way of demonstrating your value. Maybe you could provide a brief PowerPoint or Google Slides presentation. However you demonstrate or explain your value, make sure that you relate your demonstration / explanation to the specific problems that you're going to be fixing for the customer.

SPIN® Selling is a really powerful approach to selling. It provides you with a structured and logical way of running sales discussions with customers, that leads the customer along a path of opening up about problems, clarifying the implication of these problems, and understanding the true commercial value of the product and service that you offer.

In preparing for your meeting, using the research you've already done into the customer's business, draw up a list of questions you might use for each of the SPIN® stages to help uncover problems you can solve. The more thought you put into preparing for the meeting, the more effective your meetings will be. As you become more familiar with the questioning techniques, you'll probably find that there are a set of questions that you use more than any others, and meeting preparation will become second nature.

A Word About Questions

Questioning skills are an absolutely vital component of effective selling. When and how you use particular types of questions will help you direct the discussion in the direction that you want. Questions typically fall into two distinct types.... "open" and "closed".

Open questions are those questions that require some form of explanation as an answer, but not a "yes" or "no" answer: "How is business right now?". "How competitive is your industry?" "How do customers react when they find invoicing errors?" Open questions are really helpful in getting customers to open up about topics or issues and their answers may lead you to ask further questions.

Closed questions are those that simply require a "yes" or "no" answer: "Are you achieving your sales targets?" "Do you find that you make errors on invoices?" Closed questions are really helpful in clarifying a specific point or for getting a customer to confirm that they have a specific problem.

Typically, during the Situation stage of your meeting your questions will mainly be "open", during the Problem and Implication and stages, you'll use a mixture of "open" and "closed" questions and during the Need Payoff stage, you'll use more "closed" questions.

We've looked at preparing for meetings, but of course, (and hopefully) sometimes you'll receive incoming phone enquiries from customers and if they're interested in talking right now, the last thing you want to do is not respond and schedule a meeting or call in the future. In these instances you don't have time to do any preparation, so it's a good idea to keep your list of SPIN® questions by the phone, so you can refer to them whilst you're talking to the customer.

You'll probably find that in the early stages of using these questioning techniques, you'll struggle to find the "right" question to ask in every situation. It takes time to become familiar with how and when to use the right questions, but practice makes perfect… the more you use the technique, the easier it will become.

If you have the capability to record your sales calls, use it! Listening back to calls you've made is an invaluable way of reviewing how the call went, and identifying alternative ways that you could have handled specific situations.

Have case studies ready to refer to during the call or send to the prospect after the call. If you don't have case studies available, think about your existing customers and how they use your product or service so that you can refer to them doing the call.

Chapter 10 - Presentations and Demonstrations

When you're engaged with a prospect, it's common to need to make some form of presentation, typically using PowerPoint or Google Slides. I imagine you've sat through hundreds of presentations over the years… I know I have! Some of them have really left an impression, others have left me struggling to stay awake.

So what are the key elements to bear in mind when you're developing a new presentation?

Firstly, decide what you want to achieve from making a presentation. Are you trying to educate a prospect? What do you want them to learn?

Secondly, put yourself in the shoes of the audience. What's going to be of most value to them?

Thirdly, what's the story you want to tell that will make the audience remember what you've talked about? What are the steps you'll take during that story?

Many salespeople completely miss the point of presentations; they think that the more they can cover about their company and their products and services, the more effective it will be. As a result, their presentations grow and grow; I've sat through some that consist of 50 or 60 slides. It makes me yawn even thinking about it.

If that's how you present, then you're not helping yourself win the sale. Your prospect will be bored senseless. They'll see you as just another salesperson delivering a pitch. You won't stand out from all the rest.

Try and keep your presentation material to 10 slides or less. If you really think you need to have a company overview, provide a hand-out to give your prospects after the presentation.

Limit the amount of text in your slides. The more text you include, the more the audience will focus on it and they'll stop listening to what you have to say. How many presentations have you sat through, where the presenter has simply read through the text that the audience can already read for themselves? They're probably reading faster than you can talk anyway.

Instead, use pictures and images to provide context to the story that you're telling and, if you need notes to remind you of the points you want to get across, use the presenter notes capability in PowerPoint that you can see on your laptop or PC, but the audience can't.

Google "Steve Jobs Presentations"... Jobs was an absolutely master at telling a story, and his slides consisted mostly of pictures and images; they included the absolute bare minimum of text and as a result, his audiences were transfixed by the story he was telling.

Avoid "tell/selling". Act as if the prospect has already selected you and you're having your first meeting with them. When you do that, they'll be able to see themselves working with you, they'll see how you're helping them to achieve their business objectives and, they're far more likely to select you over your competition.

As you're presenting, be aware of how you're talking; both in terms of the pitch of your voice and the speed of delivery. Make sure that you're projecting your voice so that everyone in the room can hear you clearly. Make eye contact with the audience.... if you're presenting to a large group of people, gradually move your eyes around the room as you're talking. This will keep your audience more engaged and they'll feel that you're talking to them as individuals rather than just reciting a script.

If you're presenting new material; topics that you've not previously presented, practice, practice and practice again before the big day. Time yourself to see how long the presentation takes and, if necessary, adjust the content to fit the time you know you'll have available. Think back to when we talked about elevator pitches and the value of trying them out on friends, colleagues and partners. Do the same with your presentations. If you make a complete hash of things in front of colleagues, it really doesn't matter, but it will help you improve your delivery.

Practicing will help you become more familiar and comfortable with the messages you're trying to communicate. It will also help you limit the extent to which you need to rely on notes during the presentation.

If you have the means to do it, record a video of yourself making your presentation so that you can actually see and hear how you come across. If you've never seen or heard yourself on video before, be prepared for a shock. How we see and hear ourselves in our own heads is usually very, very different from how others see and hear us! Understanding their view point is incredibly valuable in fine tuning how we deliver presentations.

What you really want to achieve with your presentation is to trigger a genuine conversation with the prospect about their business objectives, key priorities and strategic initiatives and explain how your product or service helps them achieve these objectives. Nothing else!

Chapter 11 - Closing

Now we have a structured approach we can use to conduct meetings and calls with potential customers.

- We've understood the current status of the customer's business.
- We've identified the problems that they're facing.
- We've clarified the implications of those problems.
- We've clarified and confirmed the specific needs of the customer and the payoff that they'll receive by solving the problems.
- We've demonstrated how we can help the customer solve the problems they're facing.
- And we've got the customer to confirm their interest in our product or service.

At this point it's essential to agree the next steps with the customer; this is what's referred to as "closing". Closing could be as simple as asking for an order, or it could be asking the customer to commit to a particular action like taking out a free software trial, setting up a demonstration, talking to colleagues or talking to another customer who's already using our product.

There are a number of techniques we can use to "close" a meeting or sale. The close technique that you choose should be based on what you know about the prospect and the type of close you believe they will be most open to. I've listed a few effective sales closing techniques that I regularly use:

The assumptive close - This technique involves using a phrase or language that assumes the sale is a done deal. It's a more subtle approach than just asking for an order. For example, you could close with, "What day would you like to receive your delivery?"

The alternative close - Similar to the assumptive close, rather than asking for a prospect's business directly, you ask them which option they prefer. For example, you could close with, "Would you like your order delivered on Wednesday or Friday?"

The suggestion close - If you have a good rapport with the prospect and they view you as a trusted expert, a suggestion close is a good approach. You could close with, "Based on what you have told me about your operations, it sounds like it's best to receive deliveries on Fridays. Does this work for you?"

The urgency close - Creating a sense of urgency places pressure on the prospect to make a decision, especially if you have identified that the client needs to make a decision quickly and is working on a short timeline. Think of the "limited time offer" as an example. However, unlike other closing techniques, this should only be used occasionally and by experienced sales people who have a strong relationship with a client.

Multiple Cycles

If your product or service and it's business value is relatively simple, it may well be possible to go through the entire process, including getting the customer's agreement to buy in a single meeting. However, for more complex sales, you'll probably find that you need to "loop back" on the process as new issues come to light, and if (like the business we described earlier that sells printing equipment) you need to talk to several contacts within the customer's business, you'll need to work through the process with each of them individually in order to build a really compelling sales message that appeals to each individual's specific needs.

If this is the case, don't panic! Treat each discussion with individual contacts as a unique sales opportunity, use the techniques we've described and if, during subsequent discussions you uncover new problems and issues that may be relevant to contacts you've already talked to, don't be afraid to revisit them. The more you're able to build a really compelling proposition, the more likely you are to close the deal.

At the end of each meeting.... close! You may not be in a position to ask for an order, but you can ask for a commitment from the prospect to act in way that moves closer to the sale, such as agreeing to a product demonstration, arranging a meeting with the ultimate decision maker and so on.

Imagine how Gavin's meeting with Helen might have gone if he'd used the SPIN® techniques we've looked at.

"Good morning Helen, it's a pleasure to meet you. Thanks for taking the time to meet me" says Gavin. "Thanks for coming in" says Helen. "I saw a couple of your LinkedIn posts and it got me thinking. I've been thinking about changing the way we create invoices for a while, so when I got your message, I took a look at your website and thought it might be useful to see if you can help us".

"Happy to help if I can" says Gavin. "It looks like you have a pretty successful operation Helen. How are things going at the moment?"

"Oh, we're pretty busy" says Helen, "we're still growing but work can be sporadic at times and I'd like to be able to grow more"

"How much would you like to grow by?" asks Gavin. "Ideally, I'd like to grow by 20% over the next twelve months" replies Helen. Gavin thinks about this, then asks "what does that represent in terms of extra revenue and profit?" "Well, 20% extra revenue would be £50,000 in a year and that represents about £12,500 in extra profit" explains Helen.

Gavin smiles.. "it sounds like you're ambitious Helen. How many staff do you have and what does everyone do?". "We're a team of three people" says Helen. "Two graphic designers who do all the creative work, plus me. I run all the client meetings and handle all of the admin work".

'You mentioned that work can be a bit sporadic Helen. What do the designers do when the workload drops?" says Gavin. "To be honest.. nothing" Helen replies. "I've even sent them home on occasion when it's really quiet".

Gavin makes a note of all of this whilst Helen's talking. "What's stopping you from growing?" he asks. Helen laughs.. "Me really!. When I get time to visit new potential clients I'm pretty good at winning the work, but with all the admin I have to do, I just can't find the time to go out and find new work".

"What sort of admin tasks take up most of your time?" asks Gavin. "The biggest element is invoicing" says Helen."That's why I thought it might be useful to look at alternative ways of managing it. Because we do lots of small jobs, I'm spending on average an hour and a half every day raising invoices, and when I'm rushed, sometimes I make mistakes".

Gavin needs to understand a bit more about Helen's invoicing process, so he asks "how exactly do you create your invoices?". Helen pulls out an example from her invoicing file to show him. "As you can see, I use a simple spreadsheet template, add in the customer's name and address, add a description of the standard services that we've provided, along with the prices and the spreadsheet works out the total and VAT for me".

That's interesting" says Gavin. "Just so I make sure I've understood correctly, you'd like to grow the business by 20% but you don't have the time to focus on selling because you're spending an hour and a half every day raising invoices, and you occasionally make errors on the invoices you send out. And finding more work would mean that you could keep the designers busy for more of the time. Is that right?".

"Yes" says Helen. "That's exactly right".

"So if you could free up more time to sell, how much extra revenue do you think you could generate?" asks Gavin. "Like I said" says Helen, "when I get to talk to prospects, I'm pretty good at winning the business. On average, every two hours I spend talking to potential clients usually generates a design project worth £500".

"And what would happen if you could eradicate the invoicing errors?" asks Gavin. "Well, for a start" Helen replies "we'd have fewer complaints to sort out and we'd lose fewer clients as well".

"You're losing clients? How many clients do you typically lose in a year and what does that represent in revenue terms?" asks Gavin. Helen thinks.. then says "last year I think I lost four long standing clients who between them were spending about £10,000 a year".

"Ouch!" says Gavin. "That's not good!". Quickly, he calculates what the impact could be on Helen's business. "So what you're telling me is that if invoicing only took half an hour each day, you'd free up an extra hour that could be spent selling. That's 20 hours a month on selling and you'd generate £500 for each 2 hours. So over the course of a month that's £5,000 of new business... or £60,000 a year and £15,000 extra profit. On top of that, your designers would be busy for more of their time and if you could eradicate the invoicing errors, you'd avoid losing four clients in a year which would mean retaining £10,000 of revenue in a year. Is that correct?"

"I hadn't thought of it in those terms" says Helen. "That's frightening!"

Gavin smiles and opens up his laptop. "Let me show you you how I think we might be able to help you".

Gavin runs through a quick demonstration of his software. He shows Helen how to set up an invoice layout similar to the one she currently uses and adds her logo to it. Then he takes her through the process of creating customer accounts and the standard service items that she sells along with their prices. “Let’s create an invoice” says Gavin, “let’s see how quickly we can do it”.

Gavin generates a new invoice, selects a customer and adds in three service lines. The prices, VAT and total are automatically calculated. Then he hits the “send to client” button, which emails the invoice to him, just as Helen would send an invoice to one of her clients.

“Wow!” says Helen. “That was so quick and easy!”.

Gavin closes his laptop and turns back to Helen. “Can you see how our software could free up that hour a day which would allow you to get more clients and generate £60,000 of sales from new clients, whilst avoiding losing clients and retaining £10,000? When we started talking, you said that you wanted to grow by £50,000 over the next twelve months, so by using our software which, incidentally, would only cost £240 per year, you’d actually be growing by £70,000. That’s £20,000 more than your target. How does that sound?”

“That sounds amazing!” says Helen. “That would make a huge difference!”.

Gavin’s excited now. “All you need to do is subscribe on our website and you’ll be up and running in no time. Thinking about it, if you wanted to do it now, I can help you get set up while I’m still here”.

“OK.. you’ve convinced me” says Helen. “Let’s do it”.

Look back at Gavin’s conversation with Helen. He explored her situation, he uncovered problems and what the implication of solving these problems would be in the business, defined Helen’s specific needs, explained the value of his product and then closed the sale.

That's SPIN® selling in action!

Of course, not every sales call or meeting you make will be as straight forward as Gavin's, but hopefully you can now see how using a logical, step by step approach to selling helps you uncover the information you need that allows you to clearly demonstrate the value of the products and services that you provide.

Chapter 12 - Handling Objections

So now you've summarised the problems you've identified, the implications of these problems and the specific needs of the customer and got the customer to confirm that you've understood everything correctly, demonstrated the value of your solution to their problems and asked for the order using one the closing techniques we've described. Easy isn't it?

Maybe not.

For some sales discussions, you'll be able to go through this process and close straight away, but often the customer will come up with a reason why they're not ready to commit to buy your product. We call these reasons not to buy "objections".

When this happens, it may feel like you've come up against a brick wall, your mind will go into panic mode and the temptation will be to assume that you've lost the sale.

Interestingly though, objections may not just appear at the end of the SPIN® Selling process. Frequently they'll appear during a product demonstration or when you're explaining your solution to their problems. If this happens, it's important to address them immediately. The longer the potential buyer hangs on to an opinion, the stronger it becomes, and the harder it will be to overcome.

Bearing this in mind, it's actually better to welcome objections or even ask for them rather than avoiding them. Try asking questions like:

"Do you have any concerns around X?"

"Are there any reasons why this product wouldn't address your problems?"

"You seem a little worried about X. What are you thinking?"

Once you've identified an objection, give the customer a chance to talk, then summarise back to them what you've just heard; this gives you a little more thinking time and confirms that you've understood what it is that they're objecting to. Now we can dig into the underlying reasons for the objection.

Keeping notes of the objections you hear most often is also helpful. Once you know what to expect, you can devote extra time to practicing and refining your responses.

Most objections typically fall into four categories:

- Price and budget
- Competition
- Authority and ability to buy
- Need and fit

Sales Objections About Price and Budget

"It's too expensive" - Price objections are the most common type, and are sometimes even raised by prospects who have every intention of buying. Be careful with price objections; if you focus on price as a selling point, you're reducing your product to a basic commodity, so revisit the product's value.

"We don't have any budget left this year." - A variation of the "no money" objection, what your customer may actually be telling you here is that they're having cash flow issues. One way to check if this is the case is to ask if they would buy if the funds were available. If the answer is positive, then try and work with them to find additional funding, or maybe you could offer extended payment terms.

Sales Objections About the Competition

"We're already working with [Vendor X]." - A prospect who's working with a competitor may actually be a blessing in disguise. The fact that they're even talking to you means that they have some concerns about their existing supplier and that they've already recognised a need and identified a solution, so you may not need to educate them about your value. Ask them about the relationship they have with the competitor. Why did they choose this service? What's working well? What's not? Pay special attention to complaints that could be solved with your product.

"I'm locked into a contract with a competitor." - This objection is arguably the easiest competitor-related objection to handle; it's worded in a way that highlights your prospect's feeling of being trapped. See if you can come up with a creative discount to offset the cost of breaking a contract early, or demonstrate value that will make up for the remaining cost of the existing contract. At worst, ask them to commit to using your product when the current contract ends.

"I can get a cheaper version of your product somewhere else." - You need to drill down into this.... Are you in a competitive situation, where the prospect is using the threat of competition to get a better price from you or do they simply think that a similar, cheaper product can do everything they need? If they think a cheaper product will suffice, then you need to revisit your value proposition and emphasise the overall worth, not the cost.

Sales Objections About Authority or Ability to Buy

"I'm not authorised to sign off on this purchase." - Ask your prospect for the name of the right person to speak to, and ask if you can speak to them together. Try to avoid bypassing your initial contact; if they're convinced of the value of your product, you can get them to help influence the person with the authority to buy.

"I'm too busy to do anything with this now." - Ask your customer what else is a priority. If they can't, it's probably a brush-off and you should press them on precisely why they don't want to engage with you. If they do explain the other priorities, don't panic. Agree a time for a follow up call or meeting and send over helpful information in the meantime so that you keep your name front of mind.

Sales Objections About Need and Fit

"I've never heard of your company." - This is a really common objection for small businesses, especially if they operate in a market where there are one or two bigger players. Treat the objection as a request for information, so provide a very quick summary of your value proposition and reference other happy customers.

"I don't really see how your product helps me." - This tells you that they haven't understood your explanation of your product's value. Simply reconfirm the problems you've discussed and explain how your product can solve specific problems.

"We don't have the time or manpower to implement the product." - This is a really common objection for technology suppliers and unless it's handled well it can kill a sale. Depending on what product you sell, it's possible your prospect will have to add new staff or divert resources to fully take advantage of your product, and if they really can't do that, you may have to cut your losses. Perhaps you can help with the implementation process, but above all, stress the value that they'll get from using the product.

"Your product doesn't have X feature, and we need it." - If this is true, you may have to admit defeat, but first clarify precisely how valuable that particular feature would be to the prospect. Then try suggesting a supplementary product that can be used in conjunction with yours and explore just how critical that extra feature is. It might be that the value that you **can** provide, outweighs the importance of the missing feature.

Objections that are actually brush off's

"Just send me some information." - This is an opportunity to re-qualify the prospect. Say, "I'd be happy to send you some information, but I want to make sure that they're relevant. What are you interested in learning about?"

"Call me back in a few months." - Prospects will often say this to avoid having to make an instant decision. Ask what's going to change between now and then as this may help you understand why they're trying to delay.

Exercise 10:

List the objections that you encounter most often, and objections that you think you might come up against, and think about ways in which you could respond to them.

Possible Objections	Response
O1. It's too expensive	Reiterate and confirm the value that my product will deliver.
O2. I'm too busy to do anything with this right now	Ask what else is a priority - could this be put back in favour of your solution. Agree a time to follow up.

O3. I can get something similar elsewhere for less money	Assess whether the alternative product actually meets all of the customer's needs. Try and identify additional value that my product would deliver that makes it more attractive than the competition
O4.	
O5.	

Remember - Objections are an inevitable part of sales. Some are legitimate reasons to walk away, whilst others are an attempt to brush you off. But as long as you're familiar with common objections and have the knowledge and skill to be able to answer them, you'll be able to distinguish between prospects who have the potential to be good customers and those you should walk away from.

Let's go back to Gavin's meeting with Helen. He's worked through the sales process and tries to close the sale..... "All you need to do is subscribe on our website and you'll be up and running in no time. Thinking about it, if you wanted to do it now, I can help you get set up while I'm still here".

Gavin can see Helen's thinking how to reply.... "I'd like some time to think about it before I make a decision" she says.

Gavin's disappointed that Helen hasn't agreed to go ahead with the subscription, and realises that he needs to understand what's making her reluctant to make a decision, so he asks "what is it that you need to think about?"

"Well" says Helen,"I don't have time right now to go through the process of setting up the customer records, service items and prices". "That's ok" Gavin replies, "I'd be happy to come back another day when you do have time. Would Tuesday morning or Thursday afternoon be more convenient?" He hopes that by using the alternative close technique, it will help Helen move towards making a commitment to go ahead.

"I'd have to check my diary first" says Helen. Gavin knows that checking her diary would be an easy thing to do, clearly there's something else that she's not telling him so he decides to confront the issue head on.

"That's fine Helen, we can schedule it whenever works for you. In the meantime, is there anything you're concerned about?"

"Well," says Helen, "I saw another invoicing software product yesterday that's cheaper than yours". Gavin knows he needs more information to be enable to handle this so he says "it's always good to look at options to make sure you're making the right decision Helen. What did you like about the product you looked at?"

"It had a really nice function that allows you to set up discounts that are automatically applied to specific customers' invoices, and I noticed that your product doesn't do that". Gavin has been looking at competitive products recently and remembers that one software vendor has this feature.

"I think I know the product you're referring to" he says. "I've heard good things about it". He's careful not to talk badly about the competition. "When we talked about your business earlier, you mentioned that most of your work consists of small design projects that are unique to each customer. How often do you apply discounts to your prices?"

"Now that you mention it" says Helen, "not very often but it does happen occasionally! We pride ourselves on the quality of our work and I'm always worried that offering discounts would suggest that we're overpricing our work".

Gavin laughs "we're exactly the same. One other thought you might want to consider" he says. "Remember that with our software, once you've created your invoice, you can automatically email it to the customer. As far as I'm aware, I don't think you can do that with the other product you've looked at. You'd have to create a pdf version of the invoice and then attach it to a separate email, and given the number of invoices you're generating, that's a lot of work. And it will only get worse as you continue to grow towards your sales objectives! So yes, you'd be paying a little more each month for our software, but you'd be saving even more time to spend on helping you grow".

"That all seems makes sense" says Helen. "OK, you've convinced me. Let's go ahead with the subscription and get started with setting up the software".

"Now?" asks Gavin, somewhat surprised that the diary issue seems to have disappeared. "Why not" Helen replies. "I was planning to do some invoicing this morning, so if you've got the time now, I can raise them in the new software".

"Of course" he replies. "it won't take long and we can get you started straight away".

Gavin smiles to himself. He's managed to uncover Helen's real concerns, addressed the threat of the competition, removed the apparent (but false) objection of Helen not having time, and closed the sale.

Hopefully now, you can see how important it is to use questions to explore around objections that you're faced with, and understand a prospect's real concerns, rather than just attacking them head on. And by understanding the relative strengths and weaknesses of your competition, and how they might apply to a prospect's business, you can build a compelling set of reasons why your product or services is the best fit for their needs.

We mentioned in Chapter 9 that it was a really useful exercise to record sales call you make, in order to review how your questioning techniques are developing over time, and the same applies to reviewing how you handle objections. The more time you spend reviewing calls and practicing how you could handle objections in different ways will help you become far more effective.

Chapter 13 - Negotiation

Wouldn't it be good if every sales call you made ended with the customer agreeing to buy from you at the price that you've quoted? For products and services with a relatively low price point, this might happen, but for most businesses it doesn't. Let's be honest, if you're buying something and spending your hard earned cash, and you thought that there was a chance you could get it for less money, you would, wouldn't you? So when you're talking to a potential customer, you think you've overcome all of their objections, they've agreed that your product provides the best solution to their problems and you've told them the price, what do you do if they ask you for a lower price, or raise another objection along the lines of "that's too expensive" or "I can't afford that"?

First of all, don't panic! It's all too easy in these circumstances to cave in and offer a lower price if you think that's going to close the sale. But if that's what you do, then a) you may be suggesting to the customer that you don't believe in the value of your product, or that you over priced it in the first place, (and that potentially damages your reputation and the relationship you've carefully built) or b) you might be agreeing to a sale for less money than you could otherwise have earned.

Negotiating is a part of business life, but it's absolutely critical to your success. Poor negotiation can damage your business just as quickly as losing key customers. If you're in the type of business where potential buyers expect to negotiate, you need to be ready for it when it happens.

So how do you go about getting what you want, when you want it, at the price that you want?

Preparation

Most negotiators have a price target or goal in mind before they start. It should be based on realistic expectations considering all the factors that will undoubtedly arise during the negotiation.

Firstly, and before you start negotiating, make sure that the buyer actually has the authority to make binding commitments. You don't want to find yourself in a position where you believe you've struck a deal, only to discover that your agreement must be approved by someone higher in the chain of command.

Secondly, and you might think this is blindingly obvious, but think carefully about what you want to walk away with.

To set yourself clear objectives, there are three key questions you should ask yourself:

1. What's the absolute best possible outcome you could achieve? Maybe it's a price of £x, deliveries phased over three months, an agreement for the customer to work with you to create a case study once they're successfully using your product, and an agreement that they'll be prepared to act as a reference for other potential customers who are thinking about buying your product.

2. What's the absolute least value that you're prepared to accept? Maybe this is a price of £x less a discount of 20%. The acid test to use is to ask yourself if you'd walk away from a sale that doesn't meet this criteria.

3. What's the most likely outcome?

Of course, you shouldn't tell the buyer what your answers are, but you need to know all of these things going in to the negotiation. Even if you're not one hundred percent sure of your answers, just having a sense of what they might be can help you. As you become clearer about each of these elements, negotiating will become easier.

Understand your strategy

There are basic principles that apply to every negotiation. The first offer that you make is the most important. It's the benchmark against which all subsequent offers will be compared. You'll never get what you don't ask for, so make your first offer a bold one..... but not a ridiculous one.

Always have something that you're prepared to give away or concede without hurting your negotiating position. Think about some nice-to-have items that aren't critical to the success of your sale, but might be of value to the buyer. Maybe that's spare parts that may or may not be needed in the end, or training to help the buyer get up and running with your product quickly. If the buyer decides to take these items out to reduce the overall cost, you haven't lost anything but it may help the buyer reach their price target. BUT.... If you know that the only way to win the sale is to provide the absolute minimum price, then this strategy may not be appropriate.

Be prepared to stop or delay the negotiation if you feel things are getting nowhere or the buyer seems stuck in their position. Indicate your reluctance to continue under those conditions and make the buyer wonder if you're just going to walk away. Try not to cave into time pressure; this can be difficult if you're overly keen to close the sale quickly, but the last thing you want is for the buyer to think that you're under pressure to finish quickly.

If the buyer rejects an offer that you've made, avoid making a new offer. Once you start down this track, you're simply giving value away and getting nothing in return. Instead, ask the buyer to propose a counter offer. This will give you an idea of the areas that they may be prepared to move on.

Remember your strengths.

Provided you've done a good job up until this point, you should know what's important to the buyer, you should know where you stand in comparison to any competitive offerings, and you should know the real commercial value that you're delivering. Restate the value as a justification for the price you've offered.

Making an offer

An offer is more than just the price of the product or service. It should include all of the elements of the sale as it will form the basis of the legally binding contract between you and your customer.

So consider including in the offer the price, elements such as the items and quantities of product that you're supplying, the scope of the offer (e.g. detailing the specific services that you're providing), the delivery schedule, any performance incentives (such as better prices for buying larger quantities within a stated timeframe), any warranties provided, and your terms and conditions.

If you think you need to give way on some element, ask for something in return; for example offering a lower price in return for the customer providing a case study. When you do offer a concession use the phrase "If you.... then I.....". For example you might say "If you can agree to a delivery date of xxx, then I can reduce the price to £x".

Show that you're reluctant to make concessions by saying things like, "I don't know if we could do X." Or "Would this work for you if we could do X?" By demonstrating reluctance, you can actually sometimes encourage the buyer to suggest an alternative.

Aim for a "Win-Win"

While you're negotiating, try to work out what you believe an acceptable outcome would be for the buyer. It may be a combination of different things that aren't necessarily tied solely to price. For example, the delivery date might be the most important thing to the other party, whilst your major selling point is product quality.

Understanding the buyer's priorities is just as important as understanding your own, so think about what you would do if you were in the buyer's shoes. Be prepared to give up the little things in exchange for the big things that you don't want to concede. Thorough preparation in understanding your limits and how far you're willing to go on all aspects of the sale will make it easier for you to think of new approaches during the negotiation.

Ultimately, your objective should be to agree a good deal without making the buyer feel that they've been pushed into a corner. This is especially true if you're likely to have to negotiate with the same buyer again in the future. And if this is the case, remember that, whatever you agree now will be expected again in the future, unless you've been careful to stipulate that the current offer is only available for this particular purchase.

Once the negotiation is finalised, you want to be able to work effectively with the customer in the future, so it's vital to find a compromise that both you and the buyer are happy with.

Closing the Deal

Always have the endgame in mind as you make offers and counter offers. If you're getting really close to an agreement but neither you or the buyer seem to be able to make that final concession, consider offering to split the difference.... provided, of course, that this doesn't take you below the absolute least value position that you'd identified during your preparation.

I was once involved in a negotiation with one of the biggest suppliers of alcoholic drinks to the retail industry. My company was asking for a price increase of 5%, but the buyers (there were two of them) were adamant that this wasn't acceptable and it felt as though anything we tried wasn't making any progress.... they didn't appear to be willing to make any sort of concession or counter offer. I knew that the buyers must have a price increase in mind that they were prepared to accept, even though their starting position had been that any increase would be unacceptable, so rather than asking what their "bottom line" increase was, I asked them if the problem was the proposed 5% increase itself. When they confirmed that yes, it was the problem, I said "If I could reduce the increase to 4.9%, would that allow you to agree the new contract day?" We agreed it there and then! That extra 0.1% concession, cost my company £10,000 but it secured a contract worth £1million per annum. A small price to pay for retaining a happy customer who trusted me and my company.

To avoid any possible misunderstandings, present your final offer in writing and include all aspects of what's been agreed. It's a good idea to keep notes of what you offered, and what you asked for in return. You wouldn't share these notes with the buyer, but they could be useful in helping you prepare for future negotiations with the same buyer, and they may help you think of ideas to use in negotiations with other customers.

Chapter 14 - Quotes And Proposals

Once you've convinced a potential customer that you have a solution to the problems that they've agreed need to be resolved, you need to make a formal offer to supply your products or services. This represents an offer which, if they formally accept, forms a legal and binding contract between you and your customer.

Depending on the complexity of your product or service and whether it's for an existing customer or a new one, this may be in the form of a simple quotation that you send with a covering email, or it might need a more complex proposal document.

However you deliver the "offer", it's useful to have a checklist of elements to include, either in a formal proposal, or in a covering email sent with a quotation. These are the components / sections I suggest you use, especially for new customers.

Background - A simple overview of the reasons behind the discussions with the customer, perhaps highlighting the number of meetings that have been held and the individuals who have been involved. List out the key topics that you identified in the situation questioning phase that in turn highlighted specific problems that the customer faces, together with the impacts that these problems have on the business. The more detail you can include which highlights the cost to the business of not solving the problems, the more powerful your solution will appear. In complex sales, this adds weight and credibility and demonstrates that you've invested a significant amount of time in exploring the customer's problems and developing an effective solution.

Customer Requirements - Include a description of the specific needs that you identified during the qualification process.

Proposed Solution - Describe the product or service that you're offering and explain how it addresses each of the specific needs identified in the Customer Requirements section.

Commercial Proposal - for simple sales this may be a quotation. In more complex sales it would usually be a separate section in the proposal document. It needs to clearly identify what the customer is buying (with quantities if relevant), the price (including VAT if relevant), the total cost, delivery timeframes and schedule (if relevant) invoicing terms (and invoicing scheduling if relevant) and the payment terms (deposits, payment dates). If, during the negotiation phase, you've used time pressure to close the sale, define what has to happen and by when in order for the price that's been offered to remain valid. Similarly, if you've agreed that the customer will agree to you generating a case study as part of your negotiation, mention this in the proposal.

You may have a separate document that sets out your Commercial Terms and Conditions, or these may be included in your standard quotation document. Whichever approach applies to your business, make sure you include them with the "offer" as this ensures that it forms part of the legal contract that you're entering into with the customer.

Return on Investment - For complex sales, it's worthwhile summarising the costs associated with not solving the identified problems, the additional value that your product will deliver and comparing this with the total cost of the solution you're offering. This highlights the real value that you're providing.

Next steps - Clearly set out what needs to happen next. It may simply be a request for the customer to reply to your email confirming that they wish to proceed, or it may be a request for the customer to place a Purchase Order with you. Alternatively, and especially if you send out large numbers of relatively standard quotations or proposals, consider investing in proposal software. This enables you to quickly create proposals, send them to the customer and the customer can electronically sign them to show their acceptance.

When you send your quotation or proposal to the customer, tell them when you plan to follow up with them. You need to give them enough time to consider the quotation or proposal and perhaps give them enough time to discuss it with colleagues, so be realistic in setting a time frame for following up. Make sure that you do actually follow up when you say you will. This demonstrates a degree of professionalism and may help you stand out from competitors if the customer is talking to more than one potential supplier.

When you do follow up, and especially if your product or service is relatively costly, don't be surprised if the customer raises new issues that haven't previously been covered, new objections or tries to negotiate a better price. If they raise new issues, simply "loop back" into the SPIN® process to re-qualify the opportunity. If they raise new objections, use the techniques we covered in Chapter 11 and if you agree a new price, then you'll need to raise and send a new quotation or proposal.

Once the customer finally agrees and confirms or places the order with you, send an email confirming receipt of the order and thank them for their business.

Chapter 15 - Account Management

The relationship with your customer doesn't end when you close the sale. Even if there's no immediate opportunity to sell something else to them, you should still make sure that you follow up with them periodically to check that they are happy with your product or service. If they raise any problems that they're having, acknowledge them and address them quickly.

Remember that losing customers is expensive. Not only do you lose the revenue that they bring, but it will take you time and effort to find new ones to replace them. If you're trying to grow your business, then it makes sense to do everything to retain the customers you've already won so that you can focus your efforts on finding new ones.

After sales service is a crucial element in maintaining a strong relationship with customers, and happy customers are more likely to buy from you again in the future. I'm sure you've had bad experiences with companies you've bought products or services from. If you're like me, then poor service companies quickly get "black listed" and you don't go back to them.

If you sell products that customers re-order on a regular basis, or you're selling products that customers subscribe to (perhaps they pay a monthly or annual subscription fee), then it's worth scheduling regular reviews with them. This gives you the opportunity to check that they're happy with the products, but also provides an opportunity to revisit the SPIN® Selling approach to see if the situational issues you first identified have changed. If they have, this might provide you with an opportunity to sell something else.

Similarly, if you're releasing new products or updating existing ones, use these as a reason to talk to your customers. Not only can you tell them about your new products, but you can explore potential opportunities to sell other products.

Assuming that the customer is happy with your product or service, and especially if you agreed this as part of the commercial package, ask if the customer would be prepared to help you develop a case study that you can use to help with sales to other customers. You could even ask if they'd be prepared to take calls from new prospects who are considering buying from you but would like to talk to existing customers before they make the commitment to buy.

Relationships and trust

Building effective and meaningful relationships with potential and existing customers is a crucial element in being successful. Your prospect needs to feel that they can trust you in every respect before they buy from you. If at any point in the sales process, they start to question what you've told them, how you relate to them, how you talk about the competition, or your understanding of their business and their objectives, you'll lose them. The main principle underpinning relationship selling is simple: Always think about the long-term impact of your actions and continue to reinforce these standards over time.

Honesty

Any demonstration of dishonesty will immediately kill a relationship. Make sure you're never misleading your customers, either by giving them false information or withholding crucial details. Don't be afraid to tell them there's something you can't do or give bad news. You'll earn their respect by telling them something isn't right before they find out for themselves.

Consistency

Be a constant presence for your clients. Interact with them on social media, like and share their postings, send them value-added emails or newsletters (provided they've "opted in" to receive them), keep them updated on any new products that you've released and even pay attention to the details of their personal lives so you can ask about their family, past-times, goals, etc. Follow up with them regularly to ask how they're getting on with your product or service. Ask if they have any questions or problems. It's much better to identify and address a problem before the customer has even flagged it to you, than have to respond to a complaint.

Go above and beyond

If you really want to secure someone's loyalty, deliver way beyond their expectations. For example, maybe you've told your contact that you'd get them tickets to your annual industry event. And you do... but in addition to the tickets, you also arrange a private meet-and-greet with a speaker you know they look up to.

Deliver on your promises

Do your best to meet every due date and commitment. Maybe you said you'd send an email connecting them to your contact by Friday. It's now 6 p.m. on Friday and you know that they won't be checking their inbox until Monday morning .... but that doesn't mean you should wait. Every time you keep your word, you bolster your trustworthiness.

Provide exclusive perks

Make your customers feel good. Tell them you're grateful for their business, ask what you can do to make them happy, make introductions for them, promote their business, maybe send them promotional gifts. Everyone loves being treated like they're special.

A sale may be a one-time event, but a relationship lasts a lifetime, and a customer who believes they have a strong and beneficial relationship with you will be a loyal customer.

Chapter 16 - Sales Activity

So far, we've looked at identifying the real commercial value that our products and services deliver, we've identified what ideal customers look like, we've considered how to start educating potential customers, how to start building relationships with them, how to assess and handle competitive threats, we've considered how customers actually buy, how to create a compelling elevator pitch, how to close, how to handle objections, how to negotiate, what should be included in a quotation or proposal and how to manage ongoing relationships with customers.

All of this takes time and, unless you're incredibly lucky, not every sales cycle that you go through will result in a sale.

Once you've decided what your sales objectives are (in Helen's case, this was increasing sales revenue by £50,000 over the next year), it's important to understand how much sales activity you need to undertake in order to achieve the objectives.

For Helen, to achieve her target of £50,000 of new sales, with an average sale being worth £500, she needs to close 100 new sales over the course of the next twelve months, **AND** make sure she doesn't lose any of her existing customers. How much selling activity does she need to do in order to hit the £50,000 target. How realistic is it that she can hit that target?

This is where really understanding in detail how you sell, the stages you go through during the sales process, how many prospects drop out at each stage, and how long the process typically takes from start to finish helps you plan the type and amount of selling activity you need to undertake in order to achieve your objectives. In addition to that, if you carefully and regularly monitor your sales activity, you'll be able to see if things are actually on track, rather than simply waiting until you start to close new sales..... or not!

That's fine of course, if you're an established business and have been monitoring your sales activity for a while, but if you've only just set up your business, there's no history of sales activity that you can work from. But it's still a useful exercise to go through to try and estimate how much activity you need to undertake to in order to assess how realistic it will be to achieve your objectives.

We'll start by thinking about the various stages we might go through from start to finish in a typical sale.

There are a myriad of different sales process models you can apply to your business, some simple, some incredibly complex depending on the nature of the products you sell and the customers you sell to, but for small businesses, I'm a great believer in keeping things as simple as possible. The process I'm going to explain is the one I use in my own business.

Firstly, we have our targeted customers or, as we'll refer to them "Prospects". These are those businesses who meet the criteria that we've decided represent an ideal customer. We attempt to connect with them on LinkedIn and Twitter, and for those that do connect, we share and comment on their postings to try and build some initial awareness and rapport. We may also have met prospects at networking events or Trade Shows.

Next, we start to approach these prospects by phone or email to try and trigger some interest in exploring how we might be able to help. Some of these prospects will respond (but not all of them) and be willing to talk by phone or face to face to explore how we might be able to help them.

We'll call these businesses who have responded "Leads". We can also include in this category those prospects who have made an incoming enquiry as they have at least some interest in what we do and offer.

Next, we talk to each of the Leads, using the SPIN® Selling techniques to understand to what extent our product or service helps them address the business problems that they're facing. As a result of these discussions, we'll find that some of the leads are a good fit for us, others won't be. This is usually referred to as "qualifying in" and "qualifying out".

Those leads that we qualify in, represent a sales "Opportunity". We've defined their business problems and specific needs, we understand how we can potentially help them, and we have a reasonable understanding of the scale, value and timeframe of the opportunity. We've also asked if the prospect wants to receive a proposal or quotation. Provided we've qualified the opportunity well, most will agree to being sent a proposal, but there may be some who don't. (If this happens, we need to revisit our SPIN® Selling techniques and re-qualify the opportunity).

Next we send a quotation or "Proposal" to those opportunities who have requested one, setting out what we're offering, the price of the offer and the value that it will deliver.

Once the proposal has been sent, there may be some negotiation, and some prospects will agree to buy ("Won"), others won't ("Lost").

So you can see, each successful or unsuccessful sale moves through 5 distinct stages from start to finish.

Prospect > Lead > Opportunity > Proposal > Won/Lost.

It takes time to move potential customers through each stage of the process, and some will drop out at each stage.

Now we need to start allocating some timescales and conversion rates to each stage in the process. Timescale refers to how long each stage typically takes. The Conversion rate refers to the proportion of potential customers in each stage who successfully move to the next stage.

Every business will be different, but let's look at an example of how this might work:

Stage	Quantity Required	Time to Progress	Conversion Rate
Prospects	100	1 week	50%
Leads	50	5 weeks	50%
Opportunities	25	2 weeks	80%
Proposal	20	2 weeks	50%
Win/Lose	10	2 weeks	

Using this example, for every 100 prospects we find, 50 of them will become leads, 25 will turn into opportunities, 20 will be sent a proposal and 10 will become customers, and typically the entire sales process will take 12 weeks from start to finish.

If these metrics are representative of Helen's business, each project she wins is typically worth £500 and each customer typically buys 2 projects in a year. To achieve her revenue growth target of £50,000 she needs to sell to 50 new customers in a year each generating £1,000 in revenue, then she needs to identify 500 prospects.

But, Helen thinks she's good at converting face to face meetings into opportunities, proposals and sales, so if she is actually as good as she says, then her activity model might look more like this:

Stage	Quantity Required	Time to Progress	Conversion Rate
Prospects	100	1 week	50%
Leads	50	5 weeks	60%
Opportunities	35	2 weeks	80%
Proposal	28	2 weeks	75%
Win/Lose	18	2 weeks	

So for every 100 prospects Helen can identify, 18 would turn into paying customers, each generating £1,000 of revenue a year; that's £18,000 of new revenue in a year. So, to achieve her sales target of £50,000 a year, she actually needs to identify around 300 prospects.

Let's update Helen's activity table showing what happens if she finds 300 prospects to approach.

Stage	Quantity Required	Time to Progress	Conversion Rate
Targeted Customers	300	1 week	50%
Prospects	150	5 weeks	60%
Opportunities	90	2 weeks	80%
Proposal	72	2 weeks	75%
Win/Lose	54	2 weeks	

But….. we also know that typically it takes a total of 12 weeks from starting to look for prospects, to closing a sale. So even if she started her new sales activity today, it would be another 12 weeks or 3 months before she closed her first new sale. So in each of the remaining 9 months of the year, she needs to win 6 new customers (54 new customers divided by 9 months).

Using this approach helps us understand how much sales activity we need to undertake in a year to achieve our sales objectives. If we break this activity down further, we can even see what we need to be doing every month or week in order to hit our target.

Activity	**Quantity required per year**	**Quantity required per month**	**Quantity required per week**
New prospects	300	25	6
New leads	150	12.5	3
New opportunities	90	7.5	2
New proposals	72	6	1.5
New customers (from month 4 onwards	54	6 (from month 4 onwards)	1.5 (from month 4 onwards)

Now Helen knows that every week, she needs to identify 6 prospects, 3 leads, 2 new opportunities, 1.5 new proposals and win 1.5 new customer (from month 4 onwards).

The advantage of breaking all of this activity down into weeks has two big advantages:

Firstly, there's a psychological effect. How much easier does it sound to Helen knowing that she needs to close 1.5 new customers compared to 54?

54 sounds like a big, scary number.... 1.5 sounds infinitely more achievable!

Secondly, by understanding what we need to be doing every week, and monitoring how we're doing against each of these activity targets, we can very easily see if we're on track. If, at the end of the first month, instead of identifying 12.5 new leads, we've only found 10, we know that we need to increase the number of prospects that we're approaching. Think of it as an early warning system. Isn't it better to know at the end of month 1 that we need to find more prospects than waiting until the end of month 4 and finding that we've only closed 2 new customers when we needed to have closed 6?

On the other hand, if we've managed to find 15 new leads in month 1, maybe we can afford to do a little less prospect research the following week (although my personal preference would be that if we're ahead of our activity targets, just keep going and look to smash our revenue targets at the end of the year).

If you're just starting your business, you won't have any of this historic information available, so make a "best guess" at the conversion rates you think you might be able to achieve, the time it might take to go from prospecting to closing, and the average value of a sale. Most importantly though, start tracking your results from day one. Over time, you'll build up a more accurate picture of how you're actually performing and you can adjust the conversion rates, time frames and average sales value to give you more realistic activity targets.

You may have heard the expression "Selling is a numbers game", and to some extent that's true... The more activity you put in, the greater the results are likely to be. But the more you also focus on the quality of activity, in terms of identifying ideal customer characteristics, building rapport and trust, effective questioning, demonstrating value, handling objections and closing effectively, the less activity you'll need to do to generate the same results.

Chapter 17 - CRM Systems

Now we've developed a sales activity model to help us work towards achieving our sales objectives. We've identified a list of prospects to communicate with, we've started to engage directly with these prospects and we've started to receive incoming enquiries which are turning into new sales leads, we're qualifying these leads and identifying sales opportunities, and we're progressing these opportunities, some of which we'll win, others we'll lose. And along the way we're sending follow up emails, making phone calls and having meetings with prospects.

That's a lot of activity to keep on top of!

You might, of course, have a phenomenal memory and be able to remember all of the prospects, leads and opportunities that you're working on. You may be able to remember all of the follow up calls and emails you need to make.

But I doubt it! I know I can't.

Maybe you could develop a sophisticated spreadsheet that tracks all the activity for you..... but I wouldn't recommend it.

To really keep on top of all your sales activity, you need to use CRM (Customer Relationship Management) software.

CRM software was originally designed to help businesses build and maintain relationships with new and existing customers. Since then, it's evolved from a simple contact management system into a sophisticated tool that can help users manage sales, marketing, point-of-sale (POS), accounting, supplier and other types of data, all in one easily accessible solution.

CRM software is used to track prospects, customers, leads, follow them up, track opportunities and nurture them through the sales pipeline. It's also used to maintain customer loyalty by storing key information to boost sales – for instance, by personalising the experience and providing excellent customer support.

There's a multitude of CRM systems out there; some free, some costly, some you access over the internet, some you install on a PC or in-house network, some designed for small teams, some for huge companies, some that link to your email and phone systems, some that automate your marketing activities, some that enable you to raise invoices and control stock items.

The range of options is huge! So where do you start?

Let's think logically about we need to be able to do to keep on top of our sales activity. And we're just focussing on sales activity here. We need to able to:

- Track our prospects and customers and all the contacts we have within each company

- Manage these relationships

- Track leads and lead activity

- Track sales opportunities to see the potential value, where we are in the sales process, the likelihood of wining the opportunity, the estimated close date and all activity related to each opportunity

- Remind us when we need to follow up prospects, leads and opportunities

- Track how successful we are at closing opportunities

- Enable us to see what's happening at any time with any prospect

- Generate Reports on our activity, results and sale forecasts
- Access our CRM data wherever we are, whenever we need it.

There are other considerations you may want to consider, but these are the basic elements that anyone in sales needs.

For more complex requirements, you might also consider:

- How long it will take to implement the software and get all the users up and running and comfortable with the new system.
- Whether the system can grow with your business and be able to adapt to your changing processes without having to be replaced?
- Whether your CRM system can link to other software you use to manage your business, such as accounting software or stock control systems? This is much less of an issue than it used to be as more and more software applications now allow you to directly connect to other systems. For example, if you're creating lots of new customer records on a regular basis, it makes sense to be able to do this in your CRM system and then, when you close the first sale, have that customer record created automatically in your accounting software so that you can immediately raise invoices. Some CRM systems will link directly to your email systems, so that whenever you send or receive emails to or from prospects, these get automatically saved against the contact record in the CRM system. This avoids an awful lot of copying and pasting.
- How many people need access to your CRM system and how much information you need to record. Most CRM software is priced per user, but some functionality (such as the number of customer records) may come at an extra cost.

All CRM software providers will offer free trials and demonstrations. Use these facilities; it will help you properly understand the pro's and con's of each product and make the selection process more effective.

Choosing the correct CRM for your business is vitally important. Thinking about the topics above will get you started, but make sure you dedicate enough time to the research process to find the best CRM tool for your business. You need to make sure that you choose the best system for your business model. Using the right CRM software will be instrumental in helping you grow your business.

No matter which system that you choose, if you have a sales team, there may be some members of your team who resist the change. I've worked with some sales people who resolutely refused to use CRM systems; they felt threatened by them, either because they thought someone else in the business might "steal" their sales opportunities or, more often, because they didn't like other people (especially their manager) being able to see exactly what they're doing day to day. Typically, if they feel threatened it's either because the business they work in has a culture of fear and/or micro-management (we'll talk about how to manage sales people in Chapter 19), or because they're not actually working as hard as they should be.

Whatever is behind the reluctance to use the CRM system, usage should be mandatory, but sell the concept to the individual by explaining the benefits to them of doing so. It will make them more efficient by automatically reminding them when contacts, leads and opportunities need to be followed up. They'll be able to see, at any time, new leads that have come in for them to follow up, how likely they are to meet their sales targets and highlight if they need to be doing more to be successful. If you do have a sales team, consider involving them in your CRM selection process to get their buy in and keeping them involved all the way through the process helps them feel less threatened by a new system. The more ownership your employees have in the selection of a new tool, the more likely they are to adopt it and help their colleagues adopt it as well.

Once you've implemented your CRM system you'll be able to track your sales process easily and accurately, and see where you are in the process at any time.

Let's take a look at how this might work in practice.

Sales Activity	**CRM Entry**
New Prospect or Lead identified	Company and contact record created
	Create a note against the contact record of any research we've conducted e.g. The type of business, what they do, who they sell to, possible business challenges, news items or articles we've seen, how we identified them etc.
	Create a task to follow up in the future.
Prospect communication (e.g. via LinkedIn or email)	Create a note against the contact of what's been sent (if your CRM integrates with your email system this may be done for you).
	Update or complete the previous task and create a new task to follow up in the future.
Follow up call / meeting held	Create a note against the contact of what was discussed, actions agreed and next steps.
	Update or complete the previous task and create a task to follow up in the future.

New Sales Opportunity identified	Create a new opportunity against the contact, showing the sales process stage, details of the products / services, estimated sale value and estimated close date.
	Update or complete the previous task and create a new task to follow up in the future.
Follow up call / meeting to progress the Opportunity	Update the Opportunity details and sales process stage as appropriate.
	Update or complete the previous task and create a new task to follow up in the future.
Prospect makes final purchase decision	Update the Opportunity to show win date and reason for win, or loss date and reason for loss.
	Update or complete previous task and create a new task to follow up in the future to see how the customer is getting on with the purchase.

To get the greatest benefit from your CRM system, it needs to be the absolute "go to" system for all day-to-day sales activities. Every single prospect, contact, email, phone call, and meeting note **MUST** be recorded and every task that's completed should be replaced with a new task. This may seem onerous to start with, but the more you use it, the more routine it will become, you'll eliminate the risk of missing an opportunity and the more effective you'll be.

Chapter 18 - Sales Commission Plans

Once you start employing sales people, you need to consider whether or not you'll be offering them a commission plan. Most successful sales people will expect to earn commission on top of their basic salary, which means that their job performance is directly linked to how much they earn. For the sales person, this means that they have more control over their earning potential.

Some commission plans are "uncapped" i.e. there's no limit to the amount of commission that can be earned, others have defined limits.

Deciding which commission structure is right for the business and also right for the sales person can be a challenge. Ultimately this depends on what it is that you want to incentivise, not just in terms of revenues generated, but also in terms of the sales behaviours that you want to encourage.

Typically, there are six types of remuneration structure you could consider for sales people:

1. Straight Salary

With this compensation method, the amount of money that can be earned each year is determined up front. An employee's pay cannot be changed unless the employment contract is re-negotiated.

Advantages: As the business owner, the salary you pay isn't impacted in any way by how the sales person performs, so you know exactly what your costs will be throughout the year.

Disadvantages: There's no incentive for the sale person to excel, so they may become complacent. Equally worrying is that if you employ a top performing salesperson, they may begin to wonder if they could earn more elsewhere.

2. Salary Plus Bonus:

Arguably, this is one of the most reliable pay structures. Under this arrangement, the sales person receives a pre-determined salary each month. At specific intervals, (typically quarterly or annually), the sales person also receives an additional fixed bonus payment if performance hits or exceeds targets.

Advantages: Your month to month employment costs are fixed and you know that you'll only have to pay more if the sales person has achieved their targets, at which point, you know the amount of the additional payment you'll need to make.

Disadvantages: Earnings for the sales person are somewhat capped. A talented employee who is a consistent over achiever may earn less with this structure than with a commission-based structure.

3. Base Salary Plus Commission

This is the most common form of compensation in sales. With this structure, a salesperson will receive a fixed annual base salary. Commission earned is based either on the amount of sales generated or, in some cases, on the gross margin that they generate. Margin based commission structures work well in businesses that buy products from one source and then "resell" them to customers.

Advantages: The sales person is guaranteed a known income from their base salary, and is incentivised to overachieve and therefore earn more. Paying commission only on the gross margin generated means that if you are unable to increase your selling price when your buying price increases, your business isn't adversely affected by having to pay commissions on static revenues whilst incurring higher costs.

Disadvantages: The commission plan needs to be carefully structured to avoid any risk of the sales person not performing consistently (i.e having some good months and some bad months).

4. Straight Commission

Straight commission means there is no base salary. An employee earns a percentage of each sale, but this is the only way to make money. This used to be very common with “door to door” type sales environments, such as double-glazing sales.

Advantages: You’ll only be paying out when sales are made, so you have no fixed costs.

Disadvantages: If the sales person has a quiet patch when they struggle to sell, or if sales cycles are typically long, then the sales person won’t earn anything at all so could quickly become disillusioned, demotivated, and potentially leave, when perhaps with some additional training or coaching (which takes time), they could have the potential to be very successful.

5. Variable Commission

Variable commission is similar to straight commission, but the rate of commission goes up and down depending on whether sales goals have been exceeded and by how much. Often the commission rate varies in “tiers”.... The sales person might receive a 5% commission on sales made over and above their target, but receive 6% on sales once they achieve 110% of target.... And so on.

Advantages: The sales person will be motivated to outperform, since the better their performance is, the more they earn. In other words, rewards are directly linked to performance.

Disadvantages: There may be a risk that the sales person ends up focusing on the quantity of sales rather than the quality of sales, (selling to bad customers, heavily discounting prices etc) meaning that customer satisfaction may not be a priority which could lead to problems later. Similarly, if the sales person is performing exceptionally well, when they approach the end of a commission period, they may try to increase their sales by reducing prices or selling to a potential bad customer in order to increase their commission earnings in the current period.

6. Residual Commission:

As long as a particular customer is generating revenue, the sales person continues to receive commission on that account every pay period. Over time, this becomes a steady income that can be relied upon.

Advantages: The sales person is incentivised to retain as many customers as possible. As their customer base grows, the amount they earn will continue to grow.

Disadvantages: Losing an account can drastically decrease the sales person's salary.

When you add a new sales person to the business, it may take time for them to build up a sales pipeline of opportunities, which means that it may be some time before they start to earn commission. If the individual you've recruited has been used to earning commission and, to some extent, has relied on commission payments, then you may want to consider making interim commission payments that will be offset against future earnings when they start to bring in sales. At the start of each pay period, an employee is advanced a specific sum of money, known as a "draw." This sum is then deducted from the commission actually earned at the end of each pay period. After paying back the draw, the sales person keeps the rest of the commission earned.

When should you pay commission?

Commission is typically paid monthly or quarterly, with perhaps an additional payment at the end of the year, but it's also worth considering at what point in the sales cycle you actually pay out. If your business is one where customers pay in advance or immediately an invoice is raised, then commission can be paid immediately the sale is made. However, if you give customers extended payment terms (e.g. paying 30 or 60 days after the date of the invoice), or if payment is spread over time (if you're delivering a project in phases), then it's probably better to delay paying commission until the customer has paid (either in part or in full). This avoids any risk of making commission payments against sales invoices that the customer doesn't actually pay and then having to "claw back" commission from sales people for bad debts.

Which commission plan is best?

When it comes to deciding on the specific commission structure you want to implement, the process is never black and white. Before you start to develop a commission structure, you need to carefully consider what it is you want to achieve. What is it that you want to incentivise the sales person to achieve and do? Ask yourself the following questions:

- How much revenue do you want the sales person to deliver?
- When do you want them to deliver it?
- How consistently do you need them to deliver sales?
- Are there particular types of customers you want your sales person to sell to?
- Is your gross margin subject to change with little or no notice?

- When do customers pay? (Do they perhaps have staged or delayed payment arrangements?)

- Do you want the sales person to focus on new customers, existing customers or a combination of both?

- When do you want to pay commission? (Monthly, quarterly, annually, or some combination).

- Do you want to restrict or even not pay commission on sales made below certain values or price points or if excessive discounts are provided?

Once you've clarified the objectives you want to achieve and the results and behaviours you want to incentivise, think about a few possible commission structures that might work for you, and then develop financial models that show how each would operate under different scenarios of sales generated. Consider what the costs and profits generated would be if the sales person failed to meet their targets, what would happen if they achieved their targets and what would happen if they significantly overachieved.

If you're not comfortable putting these models together, work with your accountant. They're ideally placed to help you develop financial models and help you think about the implications of each.

Sales Commission Reporting

In one respect, a well constructed sales commission plan drives sales people to perform and sell in a certain manner. Similarly, it also provides a structure for reporting and enables the sales person to see how their results relate to what they'll be earning. Your commission structure needs to allow you to easily review and manage it, and be flexible for any adjustments you need to make.

If your sales person can easily see how their earnings are affected by the results they generate, the more likely they are to be incentivised to perform.

Well thought out commission structures can have a major impact on the success of your sales efforts and on the success of the business, but equally if they're not planned well they can have disastrous results. Take time to consider a variety of options before you implement them. If you're introducing a new commission structure, maybe even consider implementing it for a fixed period of time (maybe three or six months), then review the results and adjust the model if required.

Chapter 19 - Hiring Sales People

So, your business is growing, you've identified the growth objectives you want to achieve over the next few years, and your sales activity model clearly shows that you can't physically do everything required to achieve those objectives. Now it's time for you to hire someone else to handle some or all of the sales activity. How and where do you find a good salesperson? What characteristics and skills should you look for? After all, as a small-business owner or start-up, you can't afford to risk your hard earned reputation by hiring the wrong person. How do you go about the hiring process?

Define the role

There's absolutely no point in starting to look for a sales person if you don't know what it is you want them to achieve.

Start by defining what you want them to generate in terms of the revenue you need. For example, you may want them to generate £100,000 of revenue in the next 12 months. How much of this will come from existing customers, how much from new ones? How many customers does this represent?

Thinking further ahead to when you have the new sales person in situ, some business owners are happy to use their business objective (in our case sales revenue of £100,000 in the first year) as the sales target for the saes person. Others will add a little more to this figure to ensure that even if the sales person doesn't quite meet their own individual target, the business overall still achieves its objectives.

There are arguments for and against each of these approaches; I've worked with some businesses who are insistent that the targets for the business should exactly match the overall business objectives, others are adamant that sales targets should be higher than the business objectives. Only you can decide which approach is most suitable for you, but whichever approach you choose, make sure that the assigned sales target, whilst ambitious, is realistic and achievable. Setting unrealistic targets is the best and quickest way of demotivating an otherwise positive sales person.

Next, break the sales target down into months; how much revenue do you want them to generate each month. This is where your sales activity model is incredibly useful in defining what's realistic. If you've been monitoring your own sales activity properly, you know the relationship and conversion ratios for prospecting activity, lead generation, opportunity identification and sales closed. You also know how long it typically takes to close a sale and you know your average sales value.

Create a sales activity model for the new role that clearly shows the level and type of activity the new person needs to do each month and week, and the results they need to achieve each month.... but again, make sure it's all realistic.

From this activity model, you can draw up a set of monthly and weekly revenue and activity targets for the new person to work towards. These are typically referred to as KPI's (Key Performance Indicators) and might include the number of new prospects to be identified each week, new leads identified, new opportunities identified and revenue generated. (We'll talk more about KPI's in Chapter 20).

How much do you plan to pay them? Will you offer some form of bonus or commission scheme that incentives them to achieve? (Refer to Chapter 18 for ideas about possible commission schemes). Look at online job adverts to check out what sort of remuneration package you'll need to offer to get the right person.

Describe the person

The next step is to think of the characteristics and skills you want the new person to bring to the role.

Where will they work? In the office? From home? Will they be mainly "on the road".

How much sales experience should they have? An experienced sales person should be able to get up to speed quickly and require less day to day support from you but will require a higher salary than someone less experienced who will need far more of your time.

What will their working hours be? Do you want someone who works 9 to 5 or is it perhaps worth considering hiring a new parent who wants to be able to work around school or child care hours, but would bring much greater experience and skills than someone new to sales working 8 hours a day? They may actually cost the same, but the greater experience and skills could generate better results than someone with less experience.

What sort of character would fit best with the culture of your business and your customers?

How much time can you afford to spend with them getting them started and helping them get their first sales?

Do you want them to have existing knowledge of your product or service? Should they have sold similar products before? Could they have sold different products but to the same sort of customers you serve?

Are there aspects of selling that you're particularly good at and want to replicate? Similarly are there aspects that you struggle with where someone with better sales skills would help you learn and develop?

What sort of personal attributes do you need? I'd suggest you want to find someone who clearly demonstrates confidence in their interpersonal dealings, someone who's self motivated, someone who will drive themselves rather than needing you to be looking over their shoulder every minute of the day. Look for someone who demonstrates conviction.. conviction in themselves, their profession, their product or service, their colleagues – pretty much in everything to do with their job. If you're trying to convince people that what you have to offer is the best thing for them, you'll have to convince yourself first. Look for someone who demonstrates real tenacity, persistence and determination; someone who doesn't get down hearted when they come up against obstacles, someone who isn't afraid to try new things, to make mistakes but learn from them. Above all you need to find someone who's a good listener, someone with excellent questioning skills who can get a prospect to open up about the problems they may be facing.

Create a Job Description

Pull of this information into a single document that describes what the new person is expected to achieve and when, what they'll be doing on a day to day basis and what experience and skills they need.

Include information about what they'll be paid, any bonus or commission they can achieve (we'll talk more about commission plans in Chapter 19), any probationary period that will apply, the notice period, what pension arrangements you provide (as an employer you have to provide a workplace pension scheme) and any other benefits you might provide such as a mobile phone, laptop computer, holidays, healthcare, gym membership etc.

Looking for Candidates

There's a whole variety of ways to find possible candidates for a new role. Some will cost you nothing but may need a fair amount of your personal time, others may require less involvement from you but will cost you more financially.

I strongly suggest you start where you shop. Start paying attention to the good salespeople you encounter when you're the buyer. What is it they're doing that makes you feel good about working with them? Learning to recognise good salespeople is the most important first step.

When you find someone who's especially good, compliment them. You might say, "You know, you have a really nice way with people." Salespeople love to be recognised and complimented.

Then, try to open the door to a conversation about whether or not they're happy at their current place of business. "I'm curious ... are you achieving what you want with this company?" If they are, again, praise and congratulate them and thank them for their service.

If they show any hesitation at all, try saying "We're growing and we're looking for a strong salesperson. If you think you might be interested, let me know. It wouldn't be right for us to talk now, while you're working. Just contact me at your convenience." Then smile and walk away.

Alternatively, ask for word-of-mouth recommendations. Tell everyone you know that you're looking for a strong salesperson. Tell your clients. If they're fans of your product, one of them might even be interested in coming on board or they might know of someone suitable. Tell your suppliers. The people who call on your business are in sales and know many others. There could be someone good they know of who's looking for a change. This can be really effective, not least because your suppliers won't recommend someone they're not convinced would be a good fit for you. Their reputation with you would be ruined and they might lose your business.

Search for potential candidates on LinkedIn. You can enter words and descriptions to search for, you can even specific locations. Consider looking at your competitors to find out who their sales people are.

Consider placing an advertisement on relevant job boards or LinkedIn.... but be very clear about the person you're seeking. Include phrases such as "self starter" or "highly motivated." Explain what your product is and the type of business you sell to. If there's a particular time of day when it's best for people to contact you, include this in the advertisement. One word of caution....... Recruitment agencies monitor this type of advertisement; after all, they're selling their services, so if you don't want them to contact you, say so. But be prepared for some of them to ignore this request!

If you're really strapped for time, then using a recruitment agency may actually be your best option. As with any type of business, there are good ones, there are bad ones..... and there are some really awful ones! Over the years I've worked with dozens, both as a hiring manager and as a potential candidate and you'll soon spot the good ones. They'll treat you as a valued customer, they'll take the time to get to know you, understand your business and it's culture, they'll offer advice on job descriptions and remuneration packages and they'll only send you CV's of candidates they think are a good fit for you. Bad ones will send you any old CV. In some recruitment businesses, the individual consultants are measured on the number of introductions and interviews they arrange as well as the placements they make. If you find an agency that operates this way... bin them immediately! You'll waste time reviewing irrelevant CV's and you may end up wasting time interviewing candidates who will never meet your requirements. When you find a good recruiter, stick with them.

Recruitment agencies normally charge a fee that's a percentage of the starting salary. Percentages will range any where from 10% to 30% of the role's starting salary and whilst it's usually true that you get what you pay for, try to negotiate a better rate.

Once you've seen a few CV's, select the ones you think look like the best options to give you a shortlist of candidates you can interview. Don't be afraid to reject candidates you don't think are a good fit; recruiting takes time and costs money, and the cost of hiring the wrong person will far outweigh the extra time you take to make sure you've found the right individual.

Preparing for interviews

Before you start interviewing any candidates, take time to carefully prepare. Think about the experience, skills and personal attributes that you identified at the beginning of the process, and draw up a list of relevant questions that you can ask candidates that will help you understand how good a fit they might be. Try to make these questions "open" as this will encourage the candidate to talk around the topic you've asked about.

It's a good idea to have a few questions prepared that get the candidate to talk about specific experiences they've had and how they've approached them. Consider questions like "tell me about a time when you were behind target and under pressure. What did you do to get back on track", or "what's the most common objection you come up against? How do you handle it?".

Interviewing

Interviewing candidates takes time and shouldn't be rushed, but there are steps you can take to minimise disruption to your day-to-day activities.

Consider holding telephone interviews as a first stage. Holding these in the evening helps you avoid disrupting your working day and in many cases it's easier for the candidates as well. Telephone interviews also give you the opportunity to assess the candidate's telephone manner. After all, that's likely to be a key aspect of how they're going to be working.

If the telephone interview goes well, ask the candidate to visit your office for a face-to-face interview. Meeting a candidate in person will give you an opportunity to see how they conduct themselves in meetings. If you already have other staff, introduce them and observe how they operate.

Over the course of the interviews, ask every candidate the same set of prepared questions and make notes of the responses you get. During the conversation, other questions will arise, but if you have a standard set of questions, it's easier to draw comparisons between the individual candidates' answers.

If you typically have to make presentations to potential customers, ask the candidates to be prepared to deliver a presentation. This could either be on a topic they understand well, or perhaps how they might approach the first 90 days in the new role. Assess how well they engage with you during the presentation. Are they keeping you interested? Do they make it interactive so that it becomes as much a discussion as a presentation, or do they simply talk "at" you? If you do ask all of them to prepare a presentation, think about what equipment you may need to provide. Will you have a projector or screen to display their slides on? Do you expect them to bring their own laptop, or should they bring their presentation on a memory stick to be used with your PC? Maybe you can ask them to email their slides to you in advance.

If you typically make product demonstrations to potential customers, ask the candidate to demonstrate their current product to you. Again, assess how they approach the challenge. Do they keep you interested? Do they attempt to identify which aspects of the product you might be most interested in and if they do this, do they focus the demonstration on these elements?

Try and avoid talking about your business too much. Firstly, you're covering a topic you already know well. Instead, ask a lot of questions and get the candidate talking so you can find out if you can work with them, if they have relevant experience, if they're reliable, and if they can express themselves well. Secondly, if they're any good at selling, they should have already research he'd your business and will have prepared a list of questions they want to ask you, in order to work out if the role is one they're interested in. It's no different to qualifying a sales opportunity.

Appointing a candidate

Once you've found a candidate who you're confident can do the job and achieve the results you need, you'll need to make a formal offer of employment. Typically this would be offered verbally first and there may be some negotiation between you and the candidate (and/or agency) to agree the final terms. If you're working with an agency, try to talk directly to the candidate rather than the agency. It will be in the agency's best interests to get the highest possible salary offer as this will be reflected in the fee that they charge you. Once the terms of employment are agreed, you'll need to confirm everything in writing and get the candidate to accept the offer in writing.

Chapter 20 - Managing Sales People

So you've hired your first sales person? Congratulations!

Now the hard work starts. If you've selected the right person, to an extent they'll manage themselves. Successful sales people are good self motivators (at least most of the time), so once they're up and running, know what they're doing day to day and are delivering the results you want, you can leave them to it......mostly.

But first we need to get them up to speed as quickly as possible.

Induction Process

The induction process is simply the means to pass as much information as possible to the new sales person in the quickest possible time in order to get them started in selling your products or services. The topics you cover with them during this process will depend entirely on the size of your business, how big your existing team is, the complexities of your product and the market that you operate in.

As a starting point you should consider covering the following topics:

- Background to your business; It's history, it's culture and it's objectives.

- The Product or Service: They need to quickly understand your product or service, it's features and benefits but most importantly, how it helps customers address the business problems they face, Also cover standard Terms & Conditions, payment terms etc. If they'll need to provide product demonstrations to prospects, get them to start preparing demonstrations and demonstrate to you.

- The market you operate in: Typical customers, the characteristics of an ideal customer, the typical challenges your customers face.

- The competition: Who they are, their relative strengths and weaknesses, your differentiators.

- Targets and KPI's: What the monthly and annual sales targets are, the monthly and weekly KPI's (taken from the sales activity model you created when you were considering whether or not to recruit for the role.

- Commission scheme: If you're implementing a commission scheme, explain how it operates, explain the rationale behind the scheme (what it is about the scheme that helps the business and incentivises the sales person), and how and when it will pay out.

- Existing Customers: Unless you're expecting the new sales person to only concentrate on generating brand new customers, they'll probably be allocated some or all of the existing customers to manage. Brief them on the background to the relationship, the key contacts in each customer, how you've helped them in the past, any current sales opportunities and consider taking the sales person to meet some of the more important customers. This will not only help educate the sales person, but with you in attendance it provides the customer with a degree of consistency meeting a new sales person and you at the same time.

- Sales Process: Explain the typical stages of a sale based on your own experience, how long a sale typically takes, what the average sales value is (although they may have already asked this during the interview process). If they've not received formal sales training in the past, consider getting them to read Neil Rackham's SPIN® Selling to provide some structure about how you operate. This will also mean you can discuss sales opportunities with a common terminology and approach.

- Reporting process: What will you expect them to report to you and how often. You may not want to have them generate a formal written monthly report, but having a key set of topics you'd like updates on each week will set some structure about what they're working on and it will give you a standard agenda to work with each time you get together. Having a weekly one to one session using an agenda like this is a good way to start. Consider including performance against KPI's, major successes achieved (major new prospects or opportunities, not just sales won), challenges faced and aspects they need assistance with.

- CRM system: How to access it, how it operates, the information they need to record, the sales process stages it incorporates and **the importance of using it constantly and consistently.**

- Administration: Access to the office (keys, access cards, opening times etc), how to book holidays or log absences, how to claim expenses incurred during their sales activity, how to raise an invoice when they make a sale (although this may actually be managed by someone else), perhaps a formal contract needs to be generated for each sale.

Don't try and cover all of these topics in one session; it's simply too much information to absorb in one go. Break it into manageable sessions (one to two hours maximum) over the first week or two to give the sales person time to reflect on what they've learned, understand the impact it has on their role, and identify any questions they may have.

Explain at the start of the induction process that you'll expect the sales person to draw up a plan that sets out what they'll be doing during the first three months and what they expect to have achieved at the end of the first 30, 60 and 90 days. This will get them to think about the structure of their working days and can form the basis of some short term objectives you can agree with them and against which they can measure themselves and which you can review with them.

The Early Days

How you manage your sales person will change over time. In the first few months you'll need to spend more time with them as they'll have numerous questions and they'll frequently encounter problems or situations they're simply not equipped to deal with. So make sure you're available and and willing to answer questions, even if you're busy doing something else.

In your weekly one to one sessions, encourage the sales person to be open and honest about how they're doing; the last thing you want is for them to not feel able to share problems with you. Problems can fester and grow over time.

Most people when faced with a new situation, especially a new job, go through a range of feelings over time. Initially they feel excited and highly motivated, but as they become more familiar with the challenges they'll encounter situations they're not familiar with, they may become worried and perhaps a little demotivated. **This is absolutely normal and just human nature**; You've probably encountered similar feelings yourself in the past. As and when this happens, explain to the sales person what's happening and reassure them that it's normal and provide as much support as you can. In these early stages you'll probably need to give them more direction about what they're doing each day, but it's worth making the effort. Once they get past this stage, they'll start to feel more comfortable with the role, they'll be asking fewer questions and you'll start to see some early successes. Over time they'll become much more self sufficient and motivated as they become familiar with all of the expectations. Different individuals will take varying amounts of time to go through this process, so constantly assess how they're feeling and continue to give guidance and reassurance as long as its required.

When They're Productive

Continue to hold the weekly one to one review sessions, but let the sales person drive the agenda so that you can provide feedback when you think it's appropriate. Try to congratulate them more than you criticise them; if you spot something they need to improve on, ask them if they've thought of different ways of approaching certain situations to encourage them to come up with ideas, rather than simply telling them what to do.

Regularly review the sales pipeline (the sales opportunities they're working on) with them to assess how well they're progressing each opportunity and review the sales forecast. All good CRM systems will allow you create a report that forecasts the likely sales results. If the forecast suggests they'll beat their targets, congratulate them and encourage them to continue the good work. If the forecast looks like it won't meet the target, work with them to understand what's missing and how they can make up the shortfall.

The CARS model

Sales people need a number of skills and capabilities to be successful. I was introduced to the **CARS** model some years ago and it's a useful, and simple way of reviewing and assessing sales performance. CARS stands for Capabilities, Activities, Results and Success.

Performance Component	Examples
Capabilities	Selling skills - Prospecting, communication, questioning, qualifying, negotiating, closing
Activity	Volume of activity, quality of activity (talking to the right type of business, the right contacts, discussing the right issues)

Results	Revenue generated, consistency of revenue generation, revenue from the right type of customer, number of customers won.

↓

SUCCESS

Combining the capabilities with the activity delivers results, which ultimately generates success.

If the sales person seems to be underperforming, work backwards through the CARS model.

If revenue targets are being missed, look at whether the sales they're making are coming from the right type of customer. Is the average sale value sufficiently high? Are they making sales consistently? Are they closing enough deals?

If the answers to most of these questions is "no", then take a close look at their activity. Are they undertaking enough activity? (this is where your weekly KPI's are invaluable). Is the quality of their activity sufficient? (Are they talking to the right type of business, the right level of contact, discussing the right issues).

If the answers to most of these questions is "yes", then it strongly suggests that their sales capabilities may be lacking, in which case, you need to review their skills in all aspects of selling - prospecting, communication, questioning, qualifying, negotiating, and closing.

Provided that you've been careful in your recruitment process, then hopefully you won't find yourself in the position of having to completely retrain someone from scratch. If you do find yourself in that position, then you need to think carefully about whether it's worth engaging a professional trainer or even replacing the sales person. Serial under performers can be a huge drain on a business; not only do they not deliver the results you want, but they can drag the motivation and enthusiasm of everyone else in the business down with them.

Motivating Sales people

It's a bit of a cliché, but managing sales teams is often compared to herding cats. They're typically strong characters, sometimes maverick, often incredibly self sufficient.

A smaller group, perhaps 20 percent of sales people, are naturally competitive and highly ambitious. These are the ones who consistently do well and hopefully these are the ones you've been able to recruit. But how do you manage everyone else? How do you get the mid-level producers to do a little more? How do you get the low-level producers to do at least something? (assuming, of course that you think it's worth investing your time to make them productive).

Motivation can be a tricky subject for managers. Different people want different things from their jobs. Some will be motivated by hard cash, others may be driven by personal satisfaction and growth, whilst others may be inspired to work hard because of the difference they are making to a customer.

In the 1950's, psychologist Frank Herzberg undertook research to try and understand employee satisfaction. He interviewed employees from a range of industries, asking them to describe situations which made them feel good and others which made them feel bad about their jobs.

The resulting report became known as Herzberg's "Motivation-Hygiene Theory". He identified certain elements that are linked to satisfaction (motivators), and others that are consistently associated with dissatisfaction (demotivators).

Motivators

Achievement – The perception that a sales person has that he or she is growing and improving.

Recognition – People love having their egos pampered.

Work itself – The best sales people simply enjoy selling. Use this motivator to your advantage. One way is to link the sales person's work to a larger goal or purpose; whether that's a personal objective or a wider social value. Help them understand why their work matters.... To them, to their colleagues, to their customers.

Increased responsibility – The desire to expand duties and authority.

Demotivators

These include company policies & procedures, supervision, working conditions and... believe it or not.... Compensation (i.e. pay)!

It's interesting isn't it? You'd think that pay was a motivator, but Herzberg's research actually found the opposite.

Herzberg calls the demotivators "hygiene factors" because hygiene is related to maintenance. In other words, good hygiene is a daily thing you should do to stay healthy. Hygiene factors, or demotivators, don't give us satisfaction or lead to better motivation, but if they're not present, they produce dissatisfaction.

In other words, compensation or pay, even if it includes commission or bonus payments, is more of a basic expectation, something you get in exchange for your work. Because of that, compensation on it's own is not enough of a differentiator to make a sales person stay at one job in preference to moving to another.

Plus, compensation is easily replaceable for top sales people. They understand that they can get paid well anywhere they go because of their talents and work habits. All of this means that if money is an equaliser, then they will look for other quality-of-life factors.

So what does this mean for you now that you're employing one or more sales people?

Firstly, you need to understand that fair and clearly communicated compensation packages are important, but they aren't in isolation enough to motivate people. Try to find ways to incorporate achievement, recognition, meaningful work and increased responsibility into the way you manage your sales team.

So, just like we ask prospective customers what's important to them, it's important to do the same with your sales people (and, to be honest, all of your employees). Find out what's important to them, what they care about and then be sensitive to what makes each person tick.

One way to keep sales people motivated, especially if you've implemented a commission structure, is to continuously help them maintain a psychological link between their success, the resulting potential earnings and a personal goal they may be trying to achieve, such as getting their first home, or going on a special holiday.

Maybe you've hired a young sales person who's aiming to save a deposit for their first house or flat. Get them to calculate how much they need to save for a deposit, how much time it will take them to earn this from commission and savings, so they have a timescale in mind, then get them to put up a picture of their ideal first home next to their computer screen as a constant reminder of what they're trying to achieve. Doing this will give them a direct and obvious link between those weekly KPI's you've agreed and their ultimate goal.... not commission, but the new flat or that fabulous holiday.

By the way, don't confuse a lack of confidence with a lack of motivation. If someone is underperforming, take time to assess whether it's a motivation issue or a confidence issue. If confidence is the problem, then use the CARS model to help understand what steps you need to take.

Above All, Celebrate Success!

Remember that successful sales people are naturally competitive and to a greater or lesser extent, driven by their egos. Having someone recognise and acknowledge their successes will continue to motivate them.

Chapter 21 - Conclusion

So there you have it...... a complete checklist to work through to make sure you're maximising the effectiveness of selling in your business. Hopefully now you understand more about:

- Defining your value to customers
- Who we should (and shouldn't) be selling to
- How to handle competition
- How customers buy
- How to develop use elevator pitches
- Making the first sales calls and meetings
- Making effective presentations
- Closing
- Handling objections
- Negotiating
- Account management
- Sales activity models
- CRM systems
- Commission plans

- Hiring sales people, and
- Managing sales people

Now it's time to put it all into practice. It won't be easy, but referring back to the relevant chapters in the book when you're unsure about a particular topic will help you become more familiar with the ideas and make them habits that become second nature.

If you're new to selling, or you've developed some selling skills by trial and error, then use this book as your starting point, but over time, develop your own variations on the ideas that I've suggested.

If you do .... that's great!

Find out what works for you, but always question what you're doing, how you're doing it and keep an open mind and be prepared to consider other ideas you come across.

HAPPY SELLING!

About The Author

Phil is a career salesman and sales manager. He's been selling for more years than he cares to remember, selling a whole range of products and services around the world.

Phil has recruited, developed and trained sales teams and derives as much satisfaction from helping sales people and teams become successful as he ever did from closing sales.

Phil sits on the General Council of BASDA, the Business Application Software Developers Association which operates through representation and collaboration to ensure that the voice of the UK business software industry is heard by some of the highest levels within UK government, policy-makers and industry media.

Phil has worked for, owned and run Small Businesses, so he understands the mindset required, the pressures faced and the pride and sometimes defensive ways in which owner / managers view their business… it is, after all "their baby".

Phil is the founder of Proten Sales Development Ltd, using all of these years of experience to help accountants to help their clients improve their sales effectiveness.

If you'd like to connect with Phil, go to www.protensd.co.uk or connect with him on LinkedIn at www.linkedin.com/in/sayersphil

To The Reader

I hope you've enjoyed reading this book and that, at least in some small way, it's helped you think about ways in which you could improve the effectiveness of your selling skills and approach.

If you have, I'd be incredibly grateful if you could visit Amazon and write a review.

When you've done that, send a screen shot to hello@protensd.co.uk and we'll sort out a free sales review for you.... Oh... and tell your accountant too!

42675497R00078

Printed in Poland
by Amazon Fulfillment
Poland Sp. z o.o., Wrocław